Barnes & Noble Critical Studies

General Editor: Anne Smith

George Gissing: Ideology and Fiction

GEORGE GISSING:
IDEOLOGY AND FICTION

John Goode

BOOKS
10 East 53d St., New York 10022
(a division of Harper & Row Publishers. Inc.)

Barnes & Noble Books
Harper & Row, Publishers, Inc.
10 East 53rd Street
New York

ISBN 0-06-492488-2

First published in the U.S.A. 1979
© 1978 by John Goode

Printed and Bound in Great Britain
MCMLXXIX

for my father, John Henry Goode

As the cities are very big
Experts have drawn maps for
Those who do not know the programme, showing clearly
The quickest way to reach
One's goal.

> (Brecht, "Poems Belonging to a Reader for Those Who Live
> in Cities")

Contents

Acknowledgements

This book, although it is not intended as an "introduction" to Gissing, is aimed at a much wider audience than one with special-ised knowledge of its subject, and so I have tried to write it as a self-contained argument without systematic reference to Gissing studies as a whole. But, of course, it is not independent of those studies, and rather than clutter the text with footnotes, I should like here to acknowledge my general debt to the scholarship of Pierre Coustillas and Jacob Korg, and to the very valuable histori-cal criticism of Maria Chialant, whose articles are regrettably not available in English, and Adrian Poole, whose *Gissing in Context* (Macmillan, 1975) has put the analysis of Gissing on the sophis-ticated plane denied him for so long. Each of these four have also, in various ways, given me a great deal of encouragement. I should also like to acknowledge the contribution to Gissing studies of John Spiers, whose Harvester Press editions of many of the novels have rectified the long standing inaccessibility of the work.

More generally, besides its pervasive reliance of the theoretical work of Antonio Gramsci and Walter Benjamin, my book has been decisively influenced by David Harvey's *Social Justice and the City* (Arnold, 1973). It would be meaningless to try to define the debt I have to all the colleagues who have, through discussion and the example of their own work, guided and encouraged me, but I should like to pay tribute to the late D. J. Gordon who first interested me in Gissing, and who taught me so much about the study of literature in general that my work must always be an inadequate inscription of his memory.

Finally, I should like to thank Mrs. Anne Beale for her highly competent typing from an often messy original, and my wife for her encouragement, criticism and patient work on the text.

9

Annotations

I have used the Harvester Press reprints of Gissing's novels whenever possible, but for ease of reference I have identified quotations
by noting the chapter from which they come in Roman numerals
in parenthesis after the quotation or after the first of a sequence
of quotations from the same chapter. When the novels are divided
into parts as well as chapters, I have indicated part and chapter
by upper case and lower case numerals respectively. Short titles
of other works used in the text are clarified by a note on their
first citation.

Publisher's Note

This book was commissioned for the Critical Studies series by the
former General Editor, Dr. Michael Egan, who now lectures at the
University of Massachusetts, Amherst.

1

The Empty Chair

1

Gissing has always had a "place", though a very small one and
hedged around with reservations and objections. He has it because
whatever else might be denied him, what has to be granted is
that nobody else could do what he did: nobody else could give
such an immediate report on working-class London in the
eighteen-eighties when the populace was beginning to erupt into
the West End once again, and the armies of the unskilled were
beginning to organise; nobody else could register so graphically
the economic oppression of the literary producer at the beginning
of the epoch of the mass media; nobody else could portray the
nagging frustrations of the lower middle-class woman, or the
self-destructive beguilement of the metropolitan whirlpool. "The
average artist stays at home in life," wrote Arnold Bennett in
what remains one of the best essays on Gissing, "Mr. Gissing has
travelled far and brought back strange and troublous tales full of
disturbing beauty."[1] That assessment is one that will be generally
acceptable, but Bennett goes further: Gissing suffers, he says,
"for his originality". Beauty and originality are not words we
readily associate with Gissing. On the contrary, all the hedging
that goes on around the accorded place has to do with the limitations of his vision, the narrow, often subjective mediations that
make Gissing sound so often like a whining snob who can only
see in the life he registers the depression that displaces any enthusiasm he might feel in a world held apart from the one in
which he works, a world of rather pedantic classicism and romantic nature worship. Limitations of vision that make any formal
originality impossible, for Gissing's "reality" holds no epiphanies,

makes no challenge to the imagination to find appropriate forms of expression, keeps the writer within a linguistic register that shies away from his material and fails to demand from him any but the tired fictional structures of the traditional novel. The best that can be claimed for him is that he wrote on matters that nobody else dealt with, but this means that above all the claim that has to be made for him is that he is "representative"—that is, "central" to the intellectual history of his time.

The centrality is important, and I shall want to stress it, but others have made it clear before me (most notably Maria Chialant and Adrian Poole).[2] More specifically what I want to make a claim for is the uniqueness of Gissing, his specific effectivity. Like Bennett and Orwell,[3] I feel that it is not merely the centrality of Gissing's themes which needs to be affirmed, but the "originality" of their realisation. That is to say that I think that not only can nobody do what he does, but also that there is nobody quite like him. To put it crudely, most critics treat Gissing as a "realistic" novelist, who offers his material as a transparency, only to find that transparency is obscured or misshaped by his particular preoccupations. On the contrary, I wish to argue that Gissing could not have done what he did had it not been for the specific nature of the mediations which most people see as limiting or disabling. The mediations make for a specific kind of formal engagement with the "topics" of the novels which make them, as texts, indispensable. Of course, I don't want to claim that all of Gissing's novels are masterpieces: I simply want to discover what makes them what they are, and it is clear that what they are is not the same as what they "represent".

The specific mediations fall into two groups. In the first place, Gissing is a novelist: that is, he is a specific kind of literary producer, transforming specific material in determined conditions of production. Secondly, more generally, he is an "intellectual", that is, he has a specific function within the ideological apparatus of society. Both of these conditions constitute the determinations of his effectivity. In order to argue this, I have to find a particular method. First, if we are to define what constitutes a Gissing novel, it is no use starting at the beginning with the analysis of

14

texts which are still groping towards a distinctiveness, still full of borrowings and uncertainties. Second, if we are to analyse the specific conditions of production which determine the nature of Gissing's fiction, we have to be aware of his own consciousness of them. Now there seem to me to be two salient features of Gissing's work. In the first place, he is a novelist whose major point of reference is Dickens. I don't mean by this that Dickens was the greatest influence on him. But it is Dickens who represents the specific success in the face of which Gissing has to define himself. Towards the end of his career, Gissing's most articulate energy was directed towards a critique of Dickens— both the achievement of the texts and the example of the career. We might say that Gissing was Gissing precisely because he was not Dickens. The space in which Gissing's fiction can take shape is thus first to be marked out by the account of Dickens and what, for Gissing, he represents. Secondly, the novelist's space is marked out by the position he occupies as an intellectual for whom there are certain offered ideological functions. In a developed capitalist society, this is highly problematic since, because of the necessary divorce between theory and practice, the specific commitment of the intellectual is technically an area of "freedom". This means, for example, that it seems obvious to discuss the orientation of the writer's "world view" as though it were a collection of chosen ideas which are more or less "representative". This would lead to two possibilities both of which I feel it necessary to reject at the outset. First, we could discuss Gissing's intellectual formation purely empirically as a sequence of ideas which go to shape a more or less coherent attitude. This tells us nothing in the end, because it leaves the writer as a more or less eccentric and second-rate philosopher for whom those ideas are limitations on the empirical validity of the fictions (so we would merely end up trusting the tale and not the teller, with the result that we would have to rewrite the tales so that they could really be trusted, i.e. contained in our own ideology). Secondly, we could operate a kind of genetic transformation on Gissing's intellectual history which would make is participate in a "structure of consciousness" evident in other contemporary discourses. In other words, we could see the ideas that Gissing borrows from all the diverse and dubious sources available to him as instrumental in ordering the world within the terms available to his class-historical situation. The difficulty with this is that, especially in the case of the late nineteenth-century intellectual, the only recurrent feature of this ordering is the rationalisation of "alienation"—the use of ideas to combat the intractability of the perceived world which has no specific place to offer the intellectual. But this alienation is deceptive. It is the greatest source of comfort the intellectual has, and, as within the empiricist account, it only relates to the fiction itself as a marginal and at best disabling annotation which must be dispensed with in order to rectify the representational possibilities of the text. Walter Benjamin distinguished between the situation of the writer in production relations and the situation of the writer *vis-à-vis* production relations.[4] It is a crucial distinction but it should not be thought that a writer's intellectual formation can be divorced from his practice as a writer: in other words it is as much a part of his situation in production relations as is his inheritance of forms and possibilities of expression. We are lucky with Gissing because in itself the intellectual formation is not very interesting. A bit of positivism, corrected with Schopenhauer highly diluted by Arnoldian hellenism, which in turn has traces of aestheticism, class élitism and so on. It is eclectic, contradictory and sometimes merely silly. But this does not mean we can forget it. Gissing's "ideas" are not merely the instruments of a defensive detachment, they are also the formal mediations of his situation with regard to the ideology of his masters (those from whom he has to earn a living), and thus they are related to the given raw material which he transforms into fiction. Not surprisingly, these mediating ideas enter again and again into the novels, and two texts, *Workers in the Dawn* and *The Private Papers of Henry Ryecroft*, are effectively vehicles of an intellectual formation. But more importantly than these two, at the very centre of Gissing's career, there is a novel which rehearses the whole problematic of the intellectual and his relationship to the hegemony, *Born in Exile*.

I am seeking to identify a space—a space in which Gissing's novels can become what they are. Space is only identifiable by boundaries, and those boundaries are the determinants of a literary production—the questions of form and ideological function.

2

Towards the end of the autobiographical meditation, *The Private Papers of Henry Ryecroft*,[5] Gissing recalls the furore caused by Trollope's *Autobiography* when it was published in 1883, so near the beginning of Gissing's career:

> The surprise was so cynically sprung upon a yet innocent public. At that happy time (already it seems so long ago) the literary news set before ordinary readers mostly had reference to literary work, in the reputable sense of the term, and not, as now, to the processes of "literary" manufacture and the ups and downs of the "literary" market.
>
> ("Autumn", XXII)

The surprise is Trollope's claim that he could write according to the clock, that he could "manufacture" a text without recourse to "inspiration". The important point that Gissing is making is that Trollope's market orientation is something which heralds a new age of literature despite the damage the *Autobiography* is supposed to have done to his reputation. A world in which an editor could be surprised when Trollope asked him how many words he needed for a serial is seen to be radically different from the world of today when an eminent lawyer can pay £200 a year to have his son trained in the art of fiction (XXI). The paragraph from which I have quoted is followed by a paragraph of which the first sentence is one word—"Dickens". A decade before Trollope's autobiography, at the point at which Gissing was setting out on his literary career, Forster published *The Life*, a book which was to mean much to Gissing. There too, he says, "was a disclosure of literary methods". Dickens, as a 'shrewd and vigorous man of business", could hold his own in the fight for a just remuneration of his work better than Trollope, and he was equally "methodical". But there is all the difference between manufacture ("the measuring of so many words to the hour") and work. The picture of Dickens at work does not threaten the belief in "artistic ingenuousness and fervour"—on the contrary, it is "one of the most bracing and inspiring in literature".

That one word sentence, "Dickens" indicates very precisely his significance. Not influence—in 1887 he wrote that Charlotte

Brontë was the only English novelist entirely to his taste, and it is not difficult to see why, since she, above all registers the rebellious mind trapped within institutions that is at the centre of Gissing's fictive world. And in terms of technique, he thinks that Thackeray has a better style ("He cannot be compared with Thackeray for flow of pure idiom"—*Charles Dickens*, IX) and is the tougher realist (with his "native scorn of the untrue and the feeble", he may be "held the greatest 'realist' who ever penned fiction"—*Immortal Dickens*, IV).[6] And more than that, it must be recalled that Gissing announced himself in the press in 1885 as one of Mrs. Grundy's enemies with a tribute to Thackeray's honesty in the preface to *Pendennis*. And with these two, there is Meredith:

> By hook or by crook get hold of *Diana of the Crossways*. The book is right glorious. Shakespeare in modern English; but, mind you, to be read twice, if need be, thrice. There is a preface which is a plea for philosophic fiction, an admirable piece of writing, the English alone rendering it worthy of the carefullest pondering. More "brain-stuff" in the book, than many I have read for a long time.
>
> (Letter to Algy 24.4.1885, *Letters*, p. 156)[7]

Brontë, Thackeray, Meredith—they form a pattern of antecedents which oppose most of what Dickens represents—"philosophical", "brain stuff", these are surely the key terms. Such writers are "intellectual" novelists in the narrow colloquial sense of the term. Equally it is worth noting that he told Eduard Bertz that in comparison with Brontë, Eliot was "miserable" (*Letters to Bertz*, p. 5). Why? Surely because if George Eliot is also an intellectual, she is also too much a positivist for Gissing, and this means that he doesn't find in her the intellectual disaffection of the rebellious or the ironic.

Moreover, from the beginning, Gissing feels his modernity:

> It is fine to see how the old three volume tradition is being broken through. One volume is commonest of all. It is the new school, due to continental influence. Thackeray and Dickens wrote at enormous length, and with profusion of detail; their plan is to tell everything and leave nothing to be divined. Far more artistic, I think, is the later method of merely suggesting;

18

of dealing with episodes instead of writing biographies. The old novelist is omniscient; I think it is better to tell a story precisely as one does in real life, hinting, surmising, telling in detail what *can* be told and no more. In fact, it approximates to the dramatic mode of presentment.

(Letter to Algy, August 1885, *Letters*, p. 166)

Gissing thus places himself from the start at a strict methodological distance from his predecessors—the attack on omniscience, the belief in episodes, the adherence to the dramatic mode, such criteria will be familiar to readers of George Moore and Henry James, and the modern novel in general. Although in his later writings, Gissing becomes more sceptical about "realism" specifically, there is nothing in his work to suppose that he ever departs from these ideals at least in theory. And yet, in the end, it is precisely that unstylish, unrebellious, unintellectual, omniscient vigorous man of business that elicits his most warm attention. Not merely a critical study which surely stands up as the best book on Dickens before modern criticism began to engage with him (and it is still a better, more sensitive and sensible book than a good many recent works, "a shrewd and loving" book as John Lucas says[8]), not merely a collection of prefaces, but even what might seem to be an unrewarding task, and abridgement of Forster's *Life*. As I have suggested, the work on Dickens creates a perspective from which we can see the significance of Gissing's career, because it is Dickens who is the inevitable example.

Inevitable in a number of ways. An essay of 1901 called "Dickens in Memory" makes it clear both just how central Dickens is to Gissing and in what ways. The essay is divided into three sections which describe the significance of Dickens at different stages of Gissing's life. The first recalls the arrival in his home of *Our Mutual Friend* (in the mid-sixties when Gissing would have been under ten) which is an important event because "Charles Dickens, Alfred Tennyson—these were to me as the names of household gods" (*Immortal Dickens*, p. 2). The first reading, of *The Old Curiosity Shop* at the age of ten, is significant both because of what it does to the real world ("sights of every day transfigured in the service of romance") and because of its moral effect ("the kindliness of the author's spirit"). But it is

19

also significant for something less predictable: "Among his supreme merits is that of having presented in abiding form one of the best of our national ideals—rural homeliness." It is clear in this first section that Dickens is a household god because he is the supremely middle-class novelist, the shaper of its epistemologies and ideals in the mind of the child. Later, however, after the deaths of Dickens and Gissing's father (the rhetorical conjunction is not insignificant, both stand for a past world of values, the lost childhood), Gissing finds himself in London, and Dickens now becomes a guidebook for his experience of the city. In fact Gissing describes himself as being mainly preoccupied with "making real to my vision" the London Dickens has excited in his imagination. There is a deliberate overlapping between the sections of the essay so that, for example, the childish experience of the illustrations to *Little Dorrit* meant that "London, indefinitely remote, had begun to play the necromancer in my brain", and the second section therefore, though it describes the end of childhood, and the need to make his own way in life, is still dominated by a fictional world; it is not so much that Dickens represents London, but that London represents Dickens. But at the end of the section, a different reality asserts itself: "In time I came to see London with my own eyes, but how much better when I saw it with those of Dickens!" Equally the third section is foreshadowed by the opening of the second which begins with the picture announcing Dickens' death, "The Empty Chair". Although this is still linked with childhood (Dickens died six months before Gissing's father) and the response is one of awe, there is also "a curiosity which led me to look closely at the writing table and the objects upon it . . . and I began to ask myself how books were written, and how the men lived who wrote them". Forster's biography, which is the subject of the third section thus becomes involved with Gissing's own beginnings as a novelist. From the household god we have moved to the exemplary career: "Well, this it was that stirred me, not to imitate Dickens as a novelist, but to follow afar off his example as a worker." Thus Dickens is tied up inextricably with Gissing's own sense of his own life, with the home, as the household god, the vision, "moralities" and "aspiration" of that middle-class cloudland from which Gissing emerges, and with the "last glimpse of childhood" and what follows, the London in which he found himself alone, and with the work to which he committed himself. At the same time, if Dickens is inextricably linked with these things it is distinctively "in memory", at a distance, an essential part of the past which defines the present, an example to be followed "afar off".

This double sense of centrality and distance is what shapes the books on Dickens. Like Johnson's *Preface to Shakespeare*, Gissing begins his critical study with the establishment of his subject as a classic: "It seems possible to regard Dickens from the standpoint of posterity; to consider his career, to review his literary work, and to estimate his total activity, as belonging to an age clearly distinguishable from our own" (*Critical Study*, p. 1). But the comparison with Johnson is significant because although like Shakespeare, Dickens thus becomes a subject of general discourse, a normative example to confirm or dispute the laws of literary effectivity, the phrase "as belonging to" measures a definitive methodological distance. For Johnson, Shakespeare rises above the accidents of his age and situation by virtue of his greatness; for Gissing, Dickens's greatness is located in his age, representative of it, and because of that, a permanent register of its strengths and limitations. Partly, this just means that the *Critical Study* is an excellent case of the revolution in literary criticism brought about in the nineteenth century by such writers as Sainte Beuve, Taine and Pater, but also it is a sign immediately of Gissing's own sense of historical distance not merely as an inhibiting mediation but as a mode of understanding. Throughout his work on Dickens he insists on the need in the reader for a sense of relativity. Thus, for example, recalling the notorious comment of Oscar Wilde on the death of Little Nell we can see how imaginative and yet discriminating Gissing could be about even the embarrassing moments in Dickens: "One would like to find a place, in literary criticism, for a pathos below the universal, a pathos which is relatively true; under such a head would fall these pictures of gentle and fading childhood . . . This pathos was true for them and for their day" (*Immortal Dickens*, p. 199). But this is more than a patronising indulgence of the past, it is also a central mode of understanding. Commenting on the claim Dickens made in his preface to *Oliver Twist* that he has made "a true picture", Gissing writes:

21

Think what we may of his perfectly sincere claim, the important thing, in our retrospect, is the spirit in which he made it. After a long interval during which English fiction was represented by the tawdry unreal or the high imaginative . . . a new writer demands attention for stories of obscure lives, and tells his tale so attractively that high and low give ear. It is a step in social and political history; it declares the democratic tendency of the new age. Here is the significance of Dickens's early success, and we do not at all understand his place in English literature if we lose sight of this historic point of view.

(Immortal Dickens, p. 77)

The historical relativity is thus not merely a matter of making allowances: it is an index of the social and historical effectivity of the literary text. The historic point of view is what makes for our understanding, and this is more positive than a simple over-coming of historical obstacles. There is a passage in the preface to *Pickwick Papers* which strikingly and even paradoxically shows that for Gissing, the historic perspective does not offer a back-ground, but a basis of appreciation: "Thus came into existence an English classic—a book representative of its age, exhibiting the life and the ideals of an important class of English folk, on the threshold of the Victorian era" (*Immortal Dickens*, p. 43). That the classic status of a book should be measured by its repre-sentativeness of a particular age and a particular group shows how free Gissing is from the tendency in modern criticism from Arnold onwards to establish great literature as a canon which can be contemplated as an eternal presence, as a "tradition". Now it is important to stress this because Gissing is often regarded as having a static conception of "culture" whereby an alien present is blamed for not being a mentally idealised past (specifically the culture of classical antiquity) but, as the *Private Papers of Henry Ryecroft* make clear, he is under no illusion that the Greeks had an absolute superiority. And this has important consequences for the way in which we are to read his works. The historic specificity of Gissing's novels is not a matter of background or even context: it is the whole basis of his achievement.

Furthermore, the analysis of a literary text thus becomes, by definition, the analysis of the conditions in which it was produced and for which it is made. Thus the *Critical Study* begins with an

22

account of the era to which Dickens belongs, an "age clearly distinguishable" which makes it possible to assess his work:

> In short, Dickens's years of apprenticeship to life and literature were those which saw the rise and establishment of the Middle Class, commonly called Great—of the new power in political and social England which owed its development to coal and steam and iron mechanism.
>
> (*Critical Study*, p. 2)

It is "a time of suffering, of conflict, of expansion, of progress" (p. 3) so that it is not seen reductively but with a briefly indicated but sharply formulated sense of the historical contradictions —Chartism, for example, is "a hint that the middle-class triumph of '32 was by no means a finality, seeing that behind that great class was a class numerically at all events, much greater" (p. 4). Although Gissing does not give anything like a detailed social-historical analysis of Dickens's novels, this opening chapter is methodologically important, first by virtue of the fact, merely, that he should choose to see Dickens in "his times" from the outset, and secondly, and more importantly, that he should choose to define "his times" in terms of an incipient class hegemony, for although he affirms the mimetic importance of Dickens, the fact that he can reflect the beginnings both of "vast prosperity and wide prevalence of woe", it is pervasively in terms of Dickens's relationship to that hegemony that he sees the novels. In other words, above all, he asks the question that Benjamin would have us ask, the question of the writer's situation in the relations of production before he asks about the situation of this work *vis-à-vis* the relations of production. The contradictions of Dickens's texts are the products of that determination, and it is precisely those contradictions which make for the "accuracy" of his work.

This is not a simple matter. Dickens writes most effectively about the lower middle class and he is above all a satirist. Yet, it is precisely as "a member of this class . . . become conscious and vocal" (*Immortal Dickens*, p. 19) that he has his success. The complexities of the situation are bound up with the nature of his career—in other words, Dickens's "membership" of the hegemony is not reflected in his work but is the result of it. Hence, the combination of critical detachment and ideological adherence:

23

By birth superior to the rank of proletary, inferior to that of capitalist, this young man, endowed with original genius, and with the invincible vitality demanded for its exercise under such conditions, observed in a spirit of lively criticism, not seldom of jealousy, the class so rapidly achieving wealth and rule. He lived to become, in all externals, and to some extent in the tone of his mind, a characteristic member of this privileged society; but his criticism of its foibles, and of its grave shortcomings, never ceased. The landed proprietor of Gadshill could not forget (the great writer could never desire to forget) a miserable childhood imprisoned in the limbo of squalid London; his grudge against this memory was in essence a *class* feeling; to the end his personal triumph gratified him, however unconsciously, as a social claim.

(*Critical Study*, p. 2)

Gissing's grasp here seems to me to be remarkable, and it is so, of course, because it is so comparable with his own situation, minus the vindication of the social claim. But the dialectic of the lower middle-class consciousness of the hegemony—critical and aspiring—is one both authors shared, and the different results of that dialectic are the measure of that historical distance. Partly this is simply a matter of the developing triumph of the capitalist class. Dickens, he says later, lived to see the beginnings of plutocracy, and he would not have been able to share any of its ideals. But partly also it is a question of the relative autonomy of Dickens's fiction. In a brilliant chapter on Dickens's radicalism, Gissing makes the point that Dickens is largely ignorant of the social relations of industrial production: "A more noticeable omission from his books (if we except the one novel which I cannot but think a failure) is that of the workman at war with capital" (*Critical Study*, p. 242). At the same time, he discusses the figure of Rouncewell, the ironmaster who is "the middle-class ideal", that is "a Radical in the way of becoming a considerable capitalist". For us, he goes on, it is difficult to see why Rouncewell is a more sympathetic figure than Sir Leicester Dedlock, but for Dickens, progress is to be identified with the mental image of Rouncewell, and he himself "might easily have become a great capitalist". That is, he has the virtues of the industrial middle class, and the radicalism of that class. That is why paradoxically

24

he opposes the new poor law, because it brings within the realms of legislation and systematisation, a concern for the poor which ought to be based on personal benevolence. Industrialism constitutes virtually an absent centre in Dickens: because it is not there explicitly, Dickens is able to reflect its energies and aspirations as Christian and humane virtues. The negative aspect of this is made clear in a single sentence: "He shows us poor men who suffer under tyranny, and who exclaim against the hardship of things; but never such a representative wage earner as was then to be seen battling for bread and right" (p. 242). There is the world of difference between hardship and oppression, between the injustices and miseries of the poor, and the systematic war for survival of the wage earner. That world is what separates Dickens and Gissing.

This is obvious to the extent that in his early novels, Gissing portrays the relations of industrial production, as opposed to Dickens who is mostly concerned with landed property and commercial capital. But it goes further than this. It also affects the lower middle class from which both writers come, and thus the nature of their careers and their relationship with the audience. For Dickens is poised on the threshold of industrial capitalism— its radicalism can therefore be his because at this epoch industrial capitalism is still a question of individual enterprise, the profit of enterprise, as Marx puts it, as opposed to interest. This means that the lower middle-class producer is still in an area of self-employment to some extent, rather than an area of management (it must be admitted that Gissing does not see the radical implications of Carker, Dombey's manager). Thus the production of books is not a very different enterprise from the production of other commodities. Popularity is not merely a function of the market: excellence, even realism, as we shall see, is not a contradiction of success. And ideologically, that jealousy and memory which Gissing mentions in his account of Dickens's situation is not incompatible with the middle-class radicalism which carries the free contract into humane practice: "His saviour of society was a man of heavy purse and large heart, who did the utmost possible good in his own particular sphere. This, too, was characteristic of the age of the free contract . . ." (*Critical Study*, p. 251). Gissing rather sharply comments on the blacking factory episode which remained so important a motive of Dickens's radicalism, that it is partly important because it only lasted two years: "Imagine Charles Dickens kept in the blacking warehouse for ten years", he writes, ". . . it is only too easy, knowing the character of the man so well, to conceive what would have resulted." The same kind of point is made in a passage on the Cheerybles in *The Immortal Dickens*: "Of course they are plebeians; Dickens glories in their defects of breeding . . . (he) was the spokesman of a class in rebellion against political privilege— that middle order enriching itself at the expense of the ranks below it, and aimed through political reform at social dignity" (p. 106). There are two points to emerge from this. One is that Dickens's point of view was compatible with that of industrial capitalism, partly because he didn't understand it. The other, more important, is that this lack of understanding places his fiction outside the world of a highly systematised middle-class hegemony. The system he confronts is the dying order of feudalism and mercantilism. Thus, on the one hand, he has no sociological detachment (hence his attitude to the new poor law), and on the other he makes misery episodic. In one sense, as Gissing implies when he says that *Our Mutual Friend* appeared when Dickens was already an anachronism, the distance between Dickens and Gissing is marked by Darwin. The struggle for success and recognition, the pleas of private benevolence, the belief in reform, give way to the struggle for survival, the sense of a world in which oppression is systematic and inescapable.

The historic view means that two interconnected themes pervade Gissing's work on Dickens—the question of audience and the question of realism. There is on the face of it an apparent paradox. Appropriating Wilde's aphorism from a radically different context, he says that for Dickens "Art was art precisely because it was not nature" (*Critical Study*, p. 82) yet at the same time "he was yet possessed with a sense of the absolute reality of everything he pictured forth. Had the word been in use he must necessarily have called himself a realist" (p. 85). To some extent, what Gissing is describing is a limited "veracity". Dickens first of all has a field outside which he is less effective (he is placed, in this way, against Thackeray, Crabbe and Ebenezer Elliot who reflect different areas of social life). Secondly, he has "an unfortunate fondness for the theatre" which makes for a contrast between the effectiveness of his characterisation and the contrivances of his plots. And, of course, there is the limitation imposed on Dickens by the exigences of his audience. But these points are relatively unimportant in a more searching argument about the determinations of literary production and the capacity of art to reflect reality. Take the point about theatricality—much as Gissing deplores the melodramatic in Dickens, he can also see its function: "in the best moments it enables him to give tragic significance to the commonplace, and all through his finer work it helps to produce what one may call a romantic realism" (*Immortal Dickens*, p. 27). It suggests that Gissing is fully aware that "realism" is not a matter of literary transparency but a style like any other, and Dickens is not less veracious because he transforms a literal accuracy into a memorable fancy.

What is specifically important in Gissing is that he sees the process of transformation not, as Wilde seems to, as a free choice of the artist, but as a function of the relationship between the writer and his audience. Quoting a passage from Forster's *Life* in which Dickens reveals what he would like to do with Walter Gay but adds "Do you think it may be done, without making people angry", he comments:

> The phrase about 'making people angry' signifies much less than it would in a novelist of today. It might well have taken the form: 'Can I bring *myself* to do this thing?'
>
> (*Critical Study*, p. 89)

That is not that Dickens could falsify what he had to say, but that his conception of realism identified itself with the ideology of the audience. Elsewhere Gissing describes the realism of his own day as being not more literal but rather more combative. Because Dickens and his audience are at one, we have a fiction that is universally acceptable, but not one which is for all that less representative: "This was his task in life, to embody the better dreams of ordinary men; to fix them as bright realities, for weary eyes to look upon" (p. 95). That is the ideological function of Dickens and from that function flows the limitations and the strengths.

Let us take the limitations first, because they create, as it were, the empty space which it is Gissing's task, as a more combative

27

realist faced with a situation in which the better dreams of Dickens's audience have become dominant realities, to fill. First there is the finality of Dickens's stories: "It is all so satisfying; it so rounds off our conception of life. Nothing so abhorred by the multitude as a lack of finality in stories, a vagueness of conclusion which gives then the trouble of forming surmises" (p. 93). For Gissing, as we shall see, the only structure possible, towards which his fiction evolves, is a vagueness of conclusion, a destructuring of the rounded conception of life. Related to this is characterisation. Dickens is most highly praised for this, but also is seen to idealise characters or, more generally, in the cause of an endorsed individualism, play down the relationship of condition to character (Gissing feels sorry for Uriah Heep). Again, the distance is defined for Gissing "Do you urge that Dickens should give a cause for this evil temper? Cause there is none— save of that scientific kind which has no place in English novels" (p. 168). Finality of plot, freedom of character—Gissing will need to reverse these features in order to be able to make his own fictions—to site, in other words, the determinations of his representations not in the moral imperatives of authorial control embodying the better dreams of ordinary men, but in the biological and social imperatives on which the writer can only experiment.

More importantly, however, it is Dickens's strengths that really define Gissing's fictional situation. And this too is linked precisely with what in some recent criticism is seen as part of Dickens's theatricality, that is to say the stylization and authorial control that excludes the presentation of the so-called "inner life" of characters. Gissing could see long before the appearance of Garis's *The Dickens Theatre* that Dickens's characterisation depended very largely on an illusion of vitality established by externality of details as opposed to "analysis":

> Let us turn to his literary method. It is that of all the great novelists. To set before his reader the image so vivid in his own mind, he simply describes and reports. We have, in general a very precise and complete picture of externals—the face, the gesture, the habit. In these Dickens excels; he proves to us by sheer force of physical detail how distinct was the mental shape from which he drew. We learn the tone of voice, the trick of

utterance; he declared that every word spoken by his characters was audible to him. Then does the man reveal himself in colloquy; sometimes once for all, sometimes by degrees, in chapter after chapter—though this is seldom the case. We know these people because we see and hear them.

(*Critical Study*, p. 108)

Dickens's effect depends on the establishment of an image, a complete picture of externals and the visual impact is confirmed by speech which reveals "once for all" the character himself. Later in the same chapter, Gissing argues that the visual impact of character determines its own context: "Seeing *them*, he saw the house in which they lived, the table at which they ate, and all the little habits of their day to day life. Here is an invaluable method of illusion, if an author can adopt it" (p. 122). It is obviously the reverse of Gissing's own method where context is determinate, but he is shrewd enough to recognise that a method of illusion is not to be confused with illusionism, with the mere production of effect. On the contrary, Dickens's technique is an appropriate mimesis. At the outset of the *Critical Study*, he engages with the criticism of Dickens which sees his characters as abstractions, "embodied hypocrisy, selfishness, pride, and so on, masking as everyday mortals" (pp. 12–13). On the contrary, he argues, "I see in them, not abstractions, but men and women of such loud particularities, so aggressively individual in mind and form, in voice and habit, that they forever proclaim themselves the children of a certain country, of a certain time, of a certain rank". It is a very subtle sentence which in many ways is the key to Gissing's praise of Dickens and to his own situation *vis-à-vis* Dickens. For the assertion of the loud particularities is as potentially dismissive as that which it opposes. Henry James, indeed, in a review of *Our Mutual Friend*[9] had complained that Dickens's characters were so particular that they had no general significance. But Gissing sees that this particularity in itself is a function of their typicality: it proclaims them "children" of a historic totality, of a class whose angularity had been sharpened in "combat with menacing powers" and not refined away by "the grindstone" of education: "Precisely because his books are rich in extravagances of human nature is Dickens so true a chronicler of his day and generation" (p. 14).

29

This congruence between particularisation and externality on the one hand and typicality on the other is what constitutes Dickens's veracity, not of course an absolute veracity, but a veracity made true by the historic significance of its mode of idealisation. The aesthetic distance, which is determined by Dickens's productive situation, that is the middle-class writer who never writes down to his audience, but equally never offends them, is doubly constituted. It is first an idealisation which through humour and shading makes what would merely be repulsive in actual life, a type, even a "Platonic idea" of a social reality: "Is not the fact remarkable, that by dint . . . of *omitting* those very features which in life most strongly impress us, an artist in fiction can produce something which we applaud as an inimitable portrait? (p. 102). Secondly it is a specific mode of satire:

> There is the satire which leaves cold, or alienates, the ordinary man, either because it passes above his head, or conflicts with his cherished prejudices; and there is the satire which, by appealing to the better self,—that is, to a standard of morality which he theoretically, or in very deed, accepts,—commands his sympathy as soon as he sees its drift. What is called the "popular conscience" was on Dickens's side; and he had the immense advantage of being able to raise a hearty laugh even whilst pointing his lesson. Among the rarest of things is this thorough understanding between author and public, permitting a man of genius to say aloud with impunity that which all his hearers say within themselves dumbly, inarticulately.
>
> (p. 130)

This popular coherence is thus a matter for celebration, it is an enabling distance. Gissing is as aware as Orwell or Everett Knight[10] that Dickens's effectivity is a function of his ideological organicism, his subordination to the intellectual needs of the class for whom he writes, but this is not a limit on his realism, it is, on the contrary, its very basis. It is worth dwelling on his analysis of Pecksniff and Mrs. Gamp in *The Immortal Dickens* to demonstrate this. He begins by describing them as "denizens of a mean world" who could only be tolerable as our familiars in the realm of imagination. This is because their talk is "so perfectly indicative of character" that "we never lose the first impression of surprise and amusement". But equally this talk has "its serious

30

significance", and this significance which arises precisely out of the aesthetic appropriateness of "the perfectly indicative" is its representativeness, its historical typicality: "it represents a whole society, a phase of civilisation". Each speaker, he says is "at once an individual and a type". What is interesting here is that Gissing has already pointed out that Pecksniff and Mrs. Gamp are not central to the tangled narrative, they come to us as characters, and yet between them—if they don't help the overt moral pattern of the story—they nevertheless form an organic representativeness:

> These protagonists of the book (though not of the story) stand for incalculable forces of social corruption; as in all great studies of human nature, the artist implies more than he is aware of. Given a social order which aims before everything at material comfort, yet professes obedience to spiritual law, and midway in its battling throng appears Mr. Pecksniff; lower down, where the atmosphere is thicker and fouler, one will perceive Mrs. Gamp. They are types of a multitude given over to crass materialism, yet bound by moral formula; a people which is stupidly proud of the letter though the spirit has long ceased to have a meaning for it. In their several spheres, Pecksniff and Mrs. Gamp represent respectability—the significant name of a significant status. They are the successful, and we see how they have managed to succeed. Here is the problem of modern society reduced to its simplest terms. Life disguises the repulsive truth, complicates it with all all manner of virtues, affections, prettinesses. But a great writer presents us with two specimens of humanity, and the secret is bare to all who have eyes for it.
>
> (pp. 123–24)

There may seem to be a contradiction here: Dickens makes the repulsive entertaining and by this exposes the disguised repulsiveness of life. But that is not Gissing's confusion, it is the dialectic of the specific effectivity of art. The truest poetry is the most feigning. It is the *displacement* of the real in the mirror that enables us to see it. Dickens is entertaining his audience with its own image—we can see this if we recall that Dickens's "saint" is Rouncewell. I don't think that the point about the artist implying more than he is aware of is patronising, in the way that Lawrence's injunction to trust the tale and not the teller is (at

31

least in the way academic critics brought up on the comforting doctrine of the intentional fallacy make use of it). For although it proposes in the end two audiences, the one for whom the author writes and the one whose reading is mediated by the critic (and this is confirmed by what follows the passage quoted, for Gissing goes on to say that "we laugh so much . . . that we are litttle disposed to look below the appearances which entertain us"), they do not exist in the timeless intellectual vacuum of "objective" literary criticism. The intentional fallacy and the aesthetic to which it belongs turns the literary text into "literature"— that is it appropriates the text as raw material of an ideological production, the text becomes merely the transformed base of a secondary discourse of "meanings"—it is a process of reduction and translation, the creation of a new value from past labour worked up in the present. But Gissing's perception of what is really exposed by Dickens is carefully controlled by historical materialism (not in the technical sense of course, but in a general way). We have eyes for it because we have the stand point of posterity, the recognition of the writer's real world as a "phase of civilisation". Moreover, this historic distancing is not a natural perspective. We still laugh so much that we are not disposed to use our eyes. In other words there is the possibility of two kinds of reading—a consumption of the text and a revelation of a text through a deliberated distance. Gissing is making a point about our levels of awareness rather than about Dickens. I stress this point because it is important for an understanding of Gissing to recognise that "realism" is not something that "transcends" the ideological function of the text but is the very product of it. And more than this, that Gissing knows this. It is no accident that his best novel is about literary production. His whole work derives its strength from his awareness of his productive situation. When Dickens thought that he was telling the truth by entertaining his readers, he was neither stupid nor hypocritical, for reality is a functioning structure. Without the finality, without the ideological coherence, society and its members could not act, a literary text could not have any effectivity. Historical distance is a different mode of ideology which makes for a further specific functioning. And Gissing's distance is one that has to be worked for. We shall see that the evolution of his fiction is precisely out of the Dickens realism towards a realism (equally ideological) which incorporates that distance. The distance constitutes itself as a problematic sited between the individual and the type whose conjunction is the basis of Dickens's art.

More of this presently. For the moment I want to call attention to a further specification of Dickens's effectivity. The "phase of civilisation" represented in Mrs. Gamp's talk is "lower London at the middle of our century, uttering itself so as to be forever recognisable". We recall that in "Dickens in Memory" as well as being the point of reference of the middle-class writer's productive integration (the household god) Dickens is for the young man detached from his childhood, the guide to London. At the end of the preface to *Martin Chuzzlewit* from which I have been quoting, Gissing says "To depict London was one of the ends for which Dickens was born" (p. 139). Depiction is linked as always with production. Commenting on the untypical *Sketches by Boz* he writes, "Excellent as are these little pictures of grimy or dreary London, they do not affect us with that peculiar sense of imaginative vision which is the note of his best books, that unique power of picturesque suggestiveness which enabled Dickens to create a London previously unknown, and to make it part of the mind of his readers" (p. 26). The picturesque suggestiveness carefully balances the depiction and the "creation": it is both true and imagined, and the more true because it has had to be imagined. Later, speaking of *Oliver Twist*, Gissing makes the point clearer: "London as a place of squalid mystery and terror, of the grimly grotesque, of labyrinthine obscurity and lurid fascination, is Dickens's own; he taught people a certain way of regarding the huge city, and to this day how common it is to see London with Dickens's eyes" (p. 80). Again it is not a question of being true or false, but of teaching a way of looking which exposes the previously unknown. It insists on a relativity—there are other ways of looking, other Londons previously unknown. To define this unknown is to define Gissing's whole work, but we can indicate the point of the break, the possibility of a space into which Gissing's work can be inserted in the chapter on "Style" in the *Critical Study*. He writes about the passage on London on Sunday in *Little Dorrit* as being unrepresentative in so far as it conveys an impression modulated not by humour but by "something like a splenetic mood". The phrase must surely recall another book published in the same year as *Little Dorrit*—*Les Fleurs du Mal*. But characteristically, Dickens is not like Baudelaire, his London is not, for all its horrors, the city of spleen—thus on the fog at the opening of *Bleak House*: "this darkness visible makes one rather cheerful than otherwise, for we are spectators in the company of a man who allows nothing to balk his enjoyment of life" (p. 228). Gissing is completely aware of what Adrian Poole has called Dickens's epistemological excitement in the face of the city: "it is the property of his genius to perceive romance in the commonplace", he writes, and we note that the verb is "perceives"—it is an acknowledged aspect of Dickens's veracity. At the same time it is clearly a function of his career. Gissing's career is different, partly because he has Dickens as a model. For both writers, London is more than a theme or a setting. It is the very site of their fictive work. Gissing, at least, as we shall see, defines himself as a writer as he comes to grips with his London, a London that is shared with Dickens but which by virtue of Dickens's existence and importance, has to be a London unperceived by him. The lack of "epistemological excitement" in Gissing's London is not a simple failure, it is a product of his not being Dickens, of his recognition of himself as afar off. Dickens for Gissing is the novelist of London. To that extent he is his heir, but an heir that builds his own fictions for his own time.

The empty chair. Dickens's death is the death of Gissing's childhood. Dickens's London is the London of Gissing's youth. Dickens's career is the inspiration of his manhood. But the link of Dickens and Gissing's father is vital: the household god, the father of the child. We need to become our fathers but only can achieve this by not becoming them. Adulthood is the escape from the mirror. Or at least with the artist. He has to make his work not out of his influences, but in the space he makes between him and his predecessors. Almost uniquely for Gissing (though one might think of James and Hawthorne, Lawrence and Hardy, Yeats and Morris) there is one writer who can represent that past, by whom he can define that space. The creator of memorable individual characters, contained in stories which hold the actual in an ideological distance, the creator of a London of the "imagination", above all the writer at one with his audience. These are the

34

negations of Gissing's positivity. For he will become the creator of individuals who have no typicality, who expose the social world by their oddness of their situation, rather than the angularity of their personalities. And further, whose form of belonging is not through their representativeness but through their belonging to a group which is the true focus of Gissing's characterisation. And he will place these groups in stories which have no finality and in a London that is actual, charted, stripped of its poetic obscurity. It is a method of illusion that is based not on a sense of unity with his audience but on the contrary one that commits the writer in many different ways to being one of Mrs. Grundy's enemies.

3

I want very briefly to put this discussion in a wider context. I have been arguing that if we want to understand what makes Gissing Gissing and nobody else, we have to think of him very positively as not being Dickens. But this claims nothing for the importance of that uniqueness, the significance of the space he makes for himself. The significance lies in the fact that although it is his space, the site of his specific effectivity, it is a space with conjunctions with all the writers of his generation, notably James and Hardy. It will be obvious that I have been tacitly trying to show how Gissing's acclaim for Dickens resembles, in many ways, Lukacs's[11] praise of the classical European realists, the historical mimesis, the representation of major social forces in the writer's own epoch which is manifest in their ability to create characters at once highly individual and typical, and in their portrayal of historic movements in popular life. But there is one major difference between Gissing and Lukacs, which is that Gissing's sense of the historical relativity of literary production enable's him to see that such "realism" is the product of the particular possibilities released not by a general historical situation but by the specific determinations of the relationship between the writer and his public. For Lukacs the Revolution of 1848, revealing the contradiction between the bourgeoisie and the proletariat, creating a general "malédiction tragique"[12] in the bourgeoisie, disables the writer from realism because it forces him to choose between a specious positivism (naturalism, the replacement of the

35

typical by the average) and an equally specious subjectivism (aestheticism, the abandonment of the social responsiveness of art). There is no sense, in Lukacs, that there might be the possibility of a different productive relationship which might materially change the mimetic functions of art. Gissing is as sceptical as Lukacs about the greater objectivity of naturalism, but he understands at least its new productive function:

> Combative it was, of course, from the first. Realism, naturalism and so on signified an attitude of revolt against insincerity in the art of fiction. Go to, let us picture things as they are. Let us have done with the conventional, that is to say, with mere tricks for pleasing the ignorant and the prejudiced.
>
> ("The Place of Realism in Fiction", 1895)

Of course, it will be argued that Gissing was a part of the movement whose alienation Lukacs sees as so disabling, but I have analysed the work on Dickens in such detail precisely to indicate that if there is an alienation it is not based on illusions. Gissing understands both the enabling and the paradoxical features of Dickens's success, and, better than Lukacs, his own historical distance. For, of course, neither Gissing nor Lukacs, nor, come to that Engels (on whom Lukacs's theory is built), could have understood the mimetic strength of the classical realists except from a perspective in which they are part of posterity.

For classical realism contains two contradictions which the subsequent history of literature has both to pay for and to take account of. There is first an inner contradiction—that is within the aesthetic itself. We can see this already manifest in Belinski's classic essay "On Realistic Poetry" of 1835:

> Its distinct character consists in the fact that it is true to reality; it does not create life anew, but reproduces it, and like a convex glass, mirrors in itself, from one point of view, life's diverse phenomena, extracting from them those that are necessary to create a full, vivid, and organically unified picture.[13]

We can see that Belinski is making two demands of a work of art—that it reproduce life's diverse phenomena and that it "create" an organically unified picture. There is no contradiction in this, since the two demands are reconciled with a brilliant metaphor, that of the convex mirror which reflects within its small space the whole room, a distortion which totalises leaving nothing essential out. Thus the very organicism of a work of art, its convexity, is a product of its ability to reproduce a diversity. At the same time, the metaphor, depends on a crucial formal device, the point of view, the centre of consciousness or narrator who is, in a sense, privileged in that his individuality places him in a perspective that sees everything (that is why so much realistic fiction depends on the young man displaced, travelling, poised between many strata of society, on the Sorrels, the Rastignacs, the Chichikovs and the Nicklebys). In fact this very privilege of individuality is self-annihilating:

> Its eternal hero, the unchanging object of poetic inspiration, is a human being, an individual, independent, acting freely, a symbol of the world—its final manifestation, the attempts to understand the curious riddle of himself, the final question of his own mind, the ultimate enigma of his own curious aspirations. The key to this riddle, the answer to this question, the resolution of this problem must be full consciousness, which is the mystery, the aim and the reason for his existence.

The hero is acting freely and yet is a symbol of the world, he is in search of himself, and yet the reason for his existence is given (there is a brilliant, if reductive analysis of this self-annihilation in Everett Knight's book, A Theory of the Classical Novel). But this is not an absolute contradiction, it is only the product of a changing historical situation. For as long as the bourgeois concept of freedom (the free contract, a mode of production) is at one with the bourgeois structure of determinations (the division of labour, the appropriation of the means of production), the bourgeois hero is able to freely choose himself as a symbol of the world. The ultimate enigma of his own curious aspirations confronting the world only as a matter of status, landed property, wills, fortunes, dowries—all the dead capital which awaits his productive functioning remains identifiable with the social world itself. "Any great poet is great," Belinski writes, "because the roots of his suffering or his happiness have grown deeply in the soil of 'sociality' and history and because he is thus an organ and a representative of society, of the times and of humanity." Mirror, representative, symbol, organ, such terms articulate individuality, the free subject, as the narrator of a totality. And though this is bound up with historical awareness, we note how his times and his humanity are one. But the terms no longer work, contiguity and totality no longer articulate themselves in ideology as "consciousness" as soon as productive labour and marriage, the forms of bourgeois oppression, constrict the protagonist to a place which is more rigid than the relatively sartorial place offered by a disintegrating feudal world. It is no longer possible to postulate self-discovery as totality when what you have to discover is that you are Madame Bovary. Only certain mirrors are convex—there are other distortions, not so lucky.

This relates to the external contradiction of realism, that is its role in intellectual life as a kind of discourse. It is evident in Balzac's *Avant Propos* to the *Comédie Humaine* of 1842. Balzac complained that historians had failed to give us the real substance of history "men, women and things, i.e. people and the material representation that they give to their thought." That is to be his role as a novelist. But he is not merely a historian. He is a natural historian. Society is represented as a natural phenomenon; humanity, like animality, takes its exterior form from its milieu. This Lamarckian view of evolution, which looks on the protagonist as part of a single undifferentiated force individuated by its medium, is as much the basis of Balzac's realism as his historicism, and both are based on a concept of an absolute that materialises itself in time (history) and space (nature). The author has merely to be the secretary of society. The historical and scientific analogies for realism cannot hold in the later nineteenth century since neither the Lamarckian representation nor the Hegelian idealism hold up in the face of theoretical advances such as those of Darwin and Marx (realism thus tends to bifurcate into the historicism of Tolstoi and the naturalism of Zola).

Typicality and representativeness thus become highly problematic criteria in the latter half of the nineteenth century. But this is not because of some faint consciousness that all is not well in the bourgeois world view, it is because the conditions of production for the writer as well as for the worker become at once more clear and more oppressive. Lukacs tends to admire those writers who recognise the problem but somehow grimly stick to classical realism in spite of it all. But there were also writers who tried to make a break with the organicism of the classical realists, and some of them, Flaubert and Dostoevski, for example, Gissing clearly admired. What I want to stress however is that in his response to Dickens, Gissing has his own place in the large aesthetic disruption which takes place in European literature from the late 'fifties on. And unless we recognise this, and cease looking for the typical and the representative, and start trying to find the mode of articulation that makes Gissing's novels what they are, we shan't really see what is good and significant about them. In the passage about Dickens's presentation of London on Sunday in *Little Dorrit*, Gissing writes that it gives us an idea of what kind of novels Dickens would have written "without his humour". His humour is, of course, not just his ability to be funny, but the whole range of characteristics, optimism, pathos, sense of the grotesque which make Dickens a household god. Then Gissing adds that of course he wouldn't have written novels at all without the humour. Gissing's work on Dickens shows us what Gissing might have written if he had had, or his times had allowed him, Dickens's relationship with his audience. But then of course, he wouldn't have written them at all. The empty chair remains empty throughout Gissing's work. Without that absence, the work would not be.

NOTES

1   Bennett, *Fame and Fiction* (1901), p. 207. Bennett's essay as a whole is remarkably perceptive and important.

2   M. T. Chialant has published several articles on Gissing, all of them in *Annali*, Instituto Orientale di Napoli. The most important are: "The Odd Women di George Gissing e il movimento femminista", *Sezione Germanica*, X, 1967, pp. 155–87; "L'Intelletuale tardo-Vittoriano di fronte allo dell' industria culturale", *Anglistica*, 1974, 1, pp. 9–73; " 'Cultura' e 'Anarchia' nei romanzi proletari di George Gissing", *Anglistica*, 1975, 2, pp. 1–56.

3   Orwell, *Collected Essays, Journalism and Letters*, vol. IV, pp. 428–35.

4   Benjamin, *Understanding Brecht* (1973), p. 87.

5   *The Private Papers of Henry Ryecroft* is divided into four unnumbered parts, each with a season for title, which are then subdivided into sections. Quotations are therefore identified by an abbreviated form of the season followed by a roman numeral indicating the section.

6 Quotations in this section are from *Charles Dickens: A Critical Study* (1904) and *The Immortal Dickens: Being Critical Studies of the Works of Charles Dickens* (1924). Where no short title is indicated, the quotation is from the text previously quoted.

7 *The Letters of George Gissing to Members of His Family*, collected and arranged by Algernon and Ellen Gissing (1927); *The Letters of George Gissing to Eduard Bertz, 1887–1903*, edited by Arthur C. Young (1961).

8 Lucas, *The Melancholy Man: A Study of Dickens's Novels* (1970), pp. 4–5.

9 James, *Selected Literary Criticism*, edited by M. Shapira (1968), pp. 31–5.

10 Everett Knight, *A Theory of the Classical Novel* (1969), pp. 106–42.

11 See especially *The Historical Novel* (1962).

12 Lukacs, *Histoire et Conscience de Classe* (Paris, 1960), p. 85.

13 Belinski, "On Realistic Poetry" in Becker (ed.), *Documents of Modern Literary Realism* (Princeton, 1973), pp. 41–3. This is an extract from his essay on Gogol.

2

By Right of Intellect

As the books on Dickens offer the best focus for an understanding
of Gissing's own consciousness of his role as a novelist, so another
late text, the thinly disguised autobiographical meditation, *The
Private Papers of Henry Ryecroft*, provides the clearest starting-
point for an understanding of his intellectual formation. However,
though it would be silly to try to see the use of a fictional persona
in the book as an attempt to establish any kind of authorial distance from the values and ideas recorded in it, it would be naïve
to ignore the book's form altogether. Ryecroft is clearly Gissing,
or rather the image Gissing wants us to have of himself, but two
fictional features give this image a specific status which most
autobiographies don't have. Firstly, Ryecroft is dead. Most autobiographies have some element of self-justification, but in the case
of Ryecroft, there is no point in this, and so it is futile to pass
judgement on the ideas that are articulated or to demand consistency. It is an image which appears not to need an audience.
This is confirmed by the fact that these are *private* papers which
are not prepared for public consumption by the "author" but
by an editor who takes it on himself to arrange and expose
them:

> Assuredly, this writing was not intended for the public; and yet,
> in many a passage, I seemed to perceive the literary purpose . . .
> I imagine him shrinking from the thought of a first person
> volume; he would feel it too pretentious.

It is the editor who takes the responsibility for the book's possible
pretentiousness, and it is he who gives it its seasonal form ("I did

not like to offer a mere incondite miscellany"). Thus the private jottings of a dead man are made to form a single visible coherent image without him taking any responsibility for it.

What are the effects of this highly defensive strategy? In the first place it permits Gissing to rehearse attitudes with embarrassing indifference to their human or intellectual value, as when Ryecroft admits that intellectual detachment depends on physical comfort which can only come from a class position—the ability to live without having to work, and to employ a good housekeeper who performs all the services of a wife without making any of the demands. More importantly, it enables Gissing to establish an image of the intellectual life as an end in itself, apart from the question of its social function or standing. But this also means that if the image of Ryecroft reflects his author, it is by no means identical with him, and the form of the book stresses this. For if Ryecroft is an autonomous intellectual, private and dead, the "editor" who is Gissing, is concerned to prepare a book and to give it a form that will make it accessible. In other words he performs precisely the social function which the image of Ryecroft is bent on denying. This disjunction is made clear when, after the editorial worries and hesitations have been rehearsed, the first of Ryecroft's own papers is calmly sceptical about the social status of writers:

> And why should any man who writes, even if he writes things immortal, nurse anger at the world's neglect? Who asked him to publish? Who promised him a hearing? Who has broken faith with him?

From the outset we are thus made aware of Ryecroft's "autonomy" as a function of a certain distance, that is to say his own separation from the working editor who makes public his meditations by publishing and giving form to them. Moreover, the form itself is ahistorical, past and present, narrative and discourse are intermingled, but given shape by an eternal pattern, the seasons, which the editor finds appropriate. This shape fortifies the autonomy because it places Ryecroft's fleeting thoughts against a rhythm which goes on irrespective of social formations. And yet it is precisely the socially functioning editor who does this: the autonomy is granted, made visible, formalised for Ryecroft, just as the intellectual detachment depends on a specific social privilege. It is a highly dependent autonomy.

This sense of an apartness, dependent on its distance from what supports it is redoubled by the whole structure of the book. It is a record of Ryecroft's last days, deliberately organised in terms of an eternal form so that it can come to stand for an autonomous meditation. But through the process of memory, Ryecroft's past is present as a career, as a continuing struggle within historical time. The immutability of the present is preserved because that past is hermetically sealed off from the present: the struggle of Ryecroft's life is interrupted because he is suddenly released by an unexpected legacy. There is no process by which the past changes into the present: it is there only as memory, contrasting with the present without explaining it. And yet, of course, as we shall see, the past forms a condition by which the apartness of the present seeks to justify itself. I am an intellectual because I am not a worker; I am wise and honest because I do not seek approval through publishing; I am at one with the universe, because I am no longer struggling among other men. Ryecroft's intellectual position is made possible by a series of negations which are dramatised by the book's very form, and thus the negations are heard in the text itself.

I can show the effect of this best by looking closely at a Section of the book, Spring IV, which is too long to quote, but which will be easily accessible to the reader. I want to pay attention to the structure of the argument because it typifies the way Gissing's thinking elaborates itself. The passage begins with Ryecroft's recognition of his distance from his past self. This embraces the oppositional argument ("I should have been hard put to it to defend myself") and the recapitulation of a past experience embracing the other side of privilege ("I have hungered in the streets"). This experience is then dismissed as delusive ("Yes, but all that time I was one of the privileged classes") and what is offered in its place is a complex ratification from the present which relies on psychological support ("not erring from Nature's guidance") and on a philosophical rationalisation made up of the quintessentially Gissing amalgam of stoicism and Schopenhauer. It's an argument that rehearses other values only to insist on Ryecroft's special privilege of apartness, and out of it grows what Poole has termed "the shallow structure of desire"[1]— the strangely private utopia which combines a highly romantic "spirituality" (the cult of books and flowers) with a cynical embrace of material comforts. At the same time, the passage itself and its context show that the structure of desire is not an abstract commitment but a highly conditioned reaction. The previous section has told the story of the little boy who is frantic because he has lost sixpence, and the following is an essay based on Johnson's views on poverty. Both recognise the importance of money as a material fact and reinforce Ryecroft's experience by reference to the trap he has escaped from: "You tell me that money cannot buy the things most precious. Your commonplace proves that you have never known the lack of it."

Thus the quietist, aggressively privileged present of the book takes meaning from the double distance—past/present, persona/ editor (who has arranged the revealing context). We are wrong, I think, to look to the book for a coherent world-view by which we can identify Gissing's ideological formation. Instead we have a series of attitudes derivative from and in defence against other possibilities. The stress on calmness is not simply a bit of eclectic philosophy. It is seen to rely on circumstances which have to be exploited and to be enjoyed, and, as Ryecroft says in the section just analysed, it depends on the recognition of privilege. In other words, to judge his attitude morally as though, for him, there is a possible choice, is to fail to see that the attitude is the product of a material determination. Which is to fail to read what Ryecroft tells us. Consider what he says of the Greeks, for example. Watching harvesters at work, clearly enjoying their good health, he is led to "the old idle dream: balance of mind and body; perfect physical health combined with the fulness of intellectual vigour" (Au XVI). This makes him think of the Greeks, but he immediately dismisses the thought. For the Greeks lived in exceptional circumstances: small communities which far from constituting a stable civilisation, produced only "a succession of briefest splendours". Their intellectual life was uncluttered by anything "alien" and their reading severely limited. Moreover, their material existence was quite different from ours, "a slave holding people, much given to social amusement, and hardly knowing what we call industry". The example of Greek life, therefore, however we may prize their art, "possesses for us not the slightest value". The purpose of this is very conservative—it rationalises the division of labour in modern life. But again the context shows that it is an experiential reaction. Before it we have the recollection of the time when he managed to get out of the city and amazed himself by making a meal of blackberries, a meal that required no money. After it, there is a meditation about agricultural labour. All three sections focus explicitly on the social basis of intellectual life. More than the ideas themselves, the process of arriving at them reveals a writer for whom intellectual values are rooted in forms of material life.

This sequence is continued with a further passage on agricultural labour which takes us to the centre of Gissing's ideological position. Ryecroft begins with a realistic assessment of what agricultural labour is like as opposed to sentimental versions of it: it is, he says, "one of the most exhausting forms of toil, and, in itself, by no means conducive to spiritual development" (Au XVIII). This makes him recall Hawthorne's disillusion with work at Brook Farm—"labour is the curse of the world". At this point the argument begins to change direction. Hawthorne, he says, went too far; labour is not a curse, but "the world's supreme blessing". Hawthorne's disgust only arose because field-work was unsuitable for him and thus "reduces" him to the mental state of those agricultural workers who rebelled against country life. By now the argument has completely turned on its head and Ryecroft regrets the disappearance of the values of primitive farming in an urbanised and mechanised community. Logically, the argument is nonsense: it is saying that although agricultural labour reduces man to the level of beasts and that therefore it is natural for the labourers to seek to improve themselves, this is just a dream which is socially destructive. From a realistic assessment of what oppression means, Ryecroft withdraws from any confrontation with that recognition into a crude, aestheticised version of Young England. It is a very typical moment in Gissing— a dangerous sympathy with the oppressed met with a pessimism which turns itself into the sentimental endorsement of an oppressive system.

Those of us who from Raymond Williams on have recognised

the awareness inevitably end up dismissing Gissing for his repression of it. But I think we are wrong to. The manner of the repression is as important as the awareness. "Keep apart, keep apart, and preserve one's soul alive", Gissing had written in 1885 (*Letters*, p. 169) and we may feel that ideologically this hopeless desire constitutes the limits of his consciousness. But *Ryecroft* shows that it is also the starting-point of his fictional effectivity. Between the recognition that agricultural labour is oppressive and in itself dehumanising and the assertion that it is also the world's greatest blessing, there is a transition based not on logic or any system of abstract value but overtly class consciousness. That agricultural labour, Ryecroft says, "played a civilising part in the history of the world is merely due to the fact that, by creating wealth, it freed a portion of mankind from the labour of the plough". Here is Gissing's ideological centre: labour is oppressive, but it makes possible an escape from oppression by those who appropriate its products. In other words, civilisation is the result of privilege, and Ryecroft's whole serenity is based on the recognition and exploitation of privilege.

Part of the value of this is that the class concept of "civilisation" is never mystified (and that is true not only of this book but also of Gissing's work as a whole: Adela Waltham in *Demos* finally places her working-class husband not as philistine or brutal, but simply as belonging to another class). And I think this explains one odd thing about Gissing's conservatism and that is its apparent triviality. Every reader of Gissing's work is familiar with those tiresome moments when cultural and even moral value seems to rest on the way you pare an orange or whether you sound your aitches. At the end of the section I have been discussing, Ryecroft laments that in the new world of emancipated labour, the word "home" will come to designate merely where people are put when they are old or sick or mad. The concept of home is a pervasively celebrated value in the book, but it is a very specific and strange concept. Essentially it means a recognisable and reliable system of distances rather than a place where people try to live together (Ryecroft doubts whether people should live together and asks how many homes are free from quarrelling). His home consists of him and his housekeeper who knows when to appear, how to keep silent and how to create a world of cleanliness and order, in short makes a comfortable space into which he can simply insert himself. Home means being able to keep calm and separate, of *preserving* one's soul as though it were a given thing. It goes with the insistence on the notion of temperament. Ryecroft's anti-democratic position, for example, is never argued for—it is simply part of his nature. His nature demands privilege, a certain materiality as the base of his intellectual freedom. That is why cultural values are so often signalised by language and mannerism (look at the long and interesting defence of Puritanism in Au XX–XXII, and note the way in which it ends up with a vindication based on its verbal delicacy). Culture thus becomes a matter of belonging, of having the right space, and if you have known the pain of exile (as Ryecroft and Gissing have done), then dropped aitches are the persistent reminder of your poverty and displacement.

At the same time, the conception of the soul and its rightful home clearly constitutes a limitation. His contemporaries, James and Hardy, working from within a class position are able to question the values of that class, and in Hardy's case, at least, able to make the journey (in *Jude*) from a critical opposition to a class opposition. For Jude is both the agent of Hardy's recognition of the cultural bankruptcy of the ruling class and the representative of an aspiring working class. Gissing's "privilege" is never secure enough for that. He can see through middle class hypocrisy and satirise its essential philistinism, but always there is a choice between belonging and not belonging (that is made clear in *Isabel Clarendon*). The struggle in Ryecroft's past is the continuing perspective on the apparent complacency and triviality of his present. It is precisely because the values of privilege have been so vulnerable that he is now so possessively jealous of them. It is all very well for critics, who mostly have the security of a class position, to find this tiresome, but this is only to judge Gissing from within a class-based moralism.

But I am not just saying that we should tolerate Gissing's peculiar culturalism, his slightly *arriviste* snobbery. I am also suggesting that it constitutes the very foundation of his value. In other words, it is not a question of an awareness which is atrophied by an alienated subjectivity, but a question of a total awareness which includes that snobbery, that shallow structure

47

of desire, because it supplies a specific focus. It is important to have a novelist who knows that paring an orange properly and appreciating great literature are part of the same social privilege. Signs that this is not a naive awareness pervade *Ryecroft*. If privilege is the basis of his serenity, he knows this well enough for it to give him unease. Of poverty, he says, "I marvel that it should not abide with me to the end; it is a sort of inconsequence in Nature, and sometimes makes me vaguely uneasy through nights of broken sleep" (Sp V). This unease persists through the memories which punctuate the meditations. Ryecroft is privileged by right of intellect, but the privilege is only an accident, and this makes it impossible to see life as an organic whole. In fact one of the most telling moments of the book is when Ryecroft, who after all has what he wants in life, says "my life is over" as though the legacy, though offering him a release into life, also takes him out of life. This contradiction which is part of the book's fictional strategy emerges again and again in all the un-contained energies which punctuate the inert detachment of the overt structure. The days of poverty are lovingly recalled: politics suddenly accidently imposes itself and Ryecroft has to cope with a worrying tendency to read history books which are disturbing. The celebrated possession of privilege, the tame utopia of the detached intellectual is lit with the flickerings of oppression and struggle that constitute his past and the world outside. At one point, Ryecroft is visited by a bout of illness which threatens to destroy his calm spirituality, and he is led to ask whether he is a materialist. Of course neither Ryecroft nor Gissing are: the insistence on the material basis of the intellectual life concerns only the question of access. There is a transcendental ideal world of mind. It is simply that circumstances decide whether you can be in touch with it.

Nevertheless *Ryecroft* makes it clear that Gissing demands a materialist analysis. Negatively, this means that to judge Gissing's "ideas" is absurd. "Ideas" are used locationally as fictional motifs in a specific way, because for Gissing the world of ideas itself is a function of a class position. That is to say that it is less important to derive a world view from Gissing's work than to understand how values and attitudes define the class function of his protagonists. For the intellectual, who is Gissing's essential pro-

tagonist, does not exist in a void: he exists in a functional relationship with the whole social structure, although because of the
particular nature of that function he is required to act out his life
in an autonomous realm of cultural tensions. The three characters
of *The Private Papers of Henry Ryecroft*, the author at grass, the
struggling writer of his past and the editor who publishes his
ruminations in a coherent ideological form, through their mutual
distances, act out the predicament of the intellectual who has to
make a place for himself in a world through which and beyond
which he can see but in which he cannot avoid seeing himself.
Unlike James and Hardy, Gissing with a dogged and admittedly
sometimes crippling literalness exposes the social mechanisms
which determine the life of the mind. And the intellectual life,
though it defines itself in terms of a place (socially and physically) becomes always a career, a struggle to reach itself which is
only achieved in death. We must now see how ideas locate the
protagonist, as a set of circumstances which insist on his mobility
in the two novels which deal most explicitly with the career of
the intellectual, *Workers in the Dawn* and *Born in Exile*.

2

In *The Theory of the Avant Garde*, Renato Poggioli makes an
important distinction between what he terms the intelligentsia
and the intellectual élite, that is between the class of intellectuals
who articulate, elaborate and criticise systems of knowledge, and
the sophisticated audience of artistic production. In fact the two
groups are frequently hostile to one another because, although
the term "avant-garde" has a political origin, it is only by an
analogy hermetically sealed off from its source, that the term
has significance in the aesthetic sphere. Political radicalism can
be embraced by a proletarianised version of the intelligentsia but
the intellectual élite precisely because it it an élite cannot so be
re-classed. As far as England is concerned, this is not only true in
the realm of the avant garde, but is true in a broader sense
whether we are thinking of oppositional movements (radicalism or
experimentalism) or to hegemonic movements. There is a notorious split in English intellectual life between what we may broadly
term art and philosophy, which dates back at least as far as

Swift's attack on projectors or Johnson's absurd attempt to refute Berkeley, and it continues into the present (we have only to think of Leavis's remark that George Eliot had nothing to learn from the Positivists). In Gissing's own time, he had the spectacle of Ruskin's career which began with the vindication of Turner's innovations and ended with libelling Whistler: the aesthetician become the sage. Or even Morris who began as a member of the intellectual élite of avant garde art and ended as a member of the radical intelligentsia vigorously opposed to what was radical in literary production. We cannot explain this simply as the persistence of two "traditions" (empiricist-utilitarian-positivist and the romantic-organic-idealist) because the opposition crosses so many boundaries. Ruskin, Arnold and Morris, for example, are no more capable of understanding the art of their own time than are Spencer or Darwin. In spite of the fact that art rather than discourse is a primary source of their theoretical positions, it is always the art of the past already conceptualised, as it were, into a closed system, as a philosophical premise.

I think that this shows a fundamental feature of English intellectual life and that is that the hegemony, which is industrial capitalism whose preconditions were laid by the emergence of landed property as a capitalist enterprise from the enclosure acts onwards, demands a quarrel between methodology and ideology in order to prevent either from becoming a theoretical practice. In other words, the *suture* between aristocracy and bourgeoisie which Gramsci[2] noted as a major feature of English life is reflected in an apparent war of empiricisms, a domain of freedom which will not intervene except as an indirect support of the working of capitalist social relations. Thus although utilitarianism and romanticism are defunct by the end of the nineteenth century, the battle is fought out in duplicating battles—Forster and Moore, Lawrence and Russell, Leavis and Snow (history, as Marx said, repeats itself as farce). What is important is that it is the self-perpetuating opposition of identical twins. There are very important exceptions to this of course—I think of Mill's *Autobiography*, of the early essays of Pater, of the whole work of Hardy. But these exceptions constitute the basis of exactly what is strangely absent in English culture, a revolutionary ideology.

And Mill's radicalism, Pater's scientism and Hardy's "pessimism" have to be explained away as sports.

This perspective is absolutely crucial to Gissing because he stands on the very threshold of the organisation of the traditional intellectual which happens when this domain of freedom is institutionalised in the University, when literary production becomes literature, and utilitarianism becomes logical positivism. In the first place, he is acutely conscious of the split between the intelligentsia and the intellectual élite. And secondly, like Hardy, he stands at the very walls of the University which organises this opposition as a professional function (the social control which the University operates). This second point is really the domain of *Born in Exile*, but it is significant that his first novel is the story of a failed love affair between a young creative worker and a middle-class girl who emancipates herself in a German University by reconciling Comte and Schopenhauer (which if it is absurd shows an attempt to reach a radical theoretical position which will embrace both science and art, the world of fact and the world of idea constituted as theoretical structures). It shows Gissing fictionally and naïvely rehearsing an un-English aspiration—the marriage of the intelligentsia and the intellectual élite, but it shows him thwarted by a larger division which embraces those opposites, class relations.

Workers in the Dawn is interesting mainly because it dramatises this dual function of the intellectual—as intelligentsia and intellectual élite—at the crucial point of its confrontation with a new world. It is new socially since the novel opens up what is seen as darkest London (the opening pages offer ironically a guided tour round the sights of the neighbourhood around Whitecross Street), and the lives of the working class. And it is new historically both because a relatively safe ideology based on religion is confronted with various kinds of radical secularism, and because the novel is set around the time of the French Commune which is seen to inspire a new wave of constructive working-class organisation. The conflict appears explicitly in what the hero feels to be his double life:

> As he grew older he felt within himself the stirrings of a double life, the one, due to his natural gifts, comprehending all the in-

51

stincts, the hopes, the ambitions of the artist; the other, originating in the outward circumstances of his childhood, and not a little in the instruction directly afforded him by Mr. Tollady, or indirectly caught from the conversation of such men as Mark Challenger and John Pether, which urged him on to the labours of the philanthropist, showing him in the terribly distinct reflex of his own imagination the ever-multiplying miseries of the poor amongst whom he lived, and painting in entrancing hues the glories of such a life as his masters, self-denying even to a fault, bent solely on the one object of making the world less wretched, even though he died in the effort.

(Vol. I, xi)

If there is an intended irony in the way in which Arthur's philanthropic yearnings are expressed in terms of artistic imagination, it is not because the dichotomy is a false one (though the very fact that Gissing paints a verbal picture in order to introduce his highly philanthropic novel might lead us to suppose this), it is merely to prepare us for the inevitability of his renunciation of social commitment in the last part. What I think interesting is that Arthur's commitment to the artistic life is understood by the middle-class reformer, Helen Norman, who simply tells him that he must be true to his own nature, but totally rejected by the working-class radical, Will Noble, who sees it merely as inconsistency. Art involves, in this novel, entrance into the dominant class, a dominant class which is seen to be very largely as benighted as the working class (in fact one of the many themes of this portmanteau work is the conjunction of the two worlds through prostitution). Arthur's two teachers, Tollady the printer and Gresham the artist, are contrasted in terms of moral worth, but what remains decisive are the conditions of work that they can respectively offer. So that on the one hand, the world of intellectual enlightenment, in which Arthur learns about the mystifications of Christianity, the determinations of history and the possibilities of progress is a world of mechanical toil: "Arthur had worked away at the 'case', and was making evident progress in the art of printing. Not that he took any pleasure in the work for its own sake; being merely manual dexterity he very soon grew disgusted with it" (I, xi). On the other hand, the world of art precludes the expression of his knowledge of poverty. After he

has addressed the working man's club on the Commune in the
phase of his life in which he has chosen to go back to printing,
his friend makes an explicit claim for the other half of the double
life:

> "What do you think, Arthur?" asked Mark Challenger, as the
> two walked home together. "Isn't this better than being a
> painter, and living at somebody else's expense? Don't you feel
> that you are more of a man?"
> "You are right!" replied Arthur, "I feel ashamed of myself
> when I think of those days. What can have possessed me to
> think of being an artist? Then I should have spent my days
> and nights in useless labour, and after all been miserably de-
> pendent upon the rich and proud . . . Now I have the consola-
> tion of knowing that I work for a useful end. The newspapers
> I help to print spreads knowledge among thousands every day;
> it makes me work with energy when I think of it . . ."
>
> (II, xi)

What immediately strikes us is how clear the choice is: on the
one hand, being a painter means living at someone else's expense,
absorbing as it does the wealth created by labour. On the other
hand, raising the consciousness of the masses, a legitimate function of the intelligentsia, involves complicity with mechanical
forms of communication. Although the novel was written too
early for Morris's very different conception of art and its relation
to social change to be available, nevertheless Ruskin's idealised
version of mediaeval art, art which is integrated into the working
life of the community, not parasitically preserving its own autonomy, was very much in the air. And when Gissing did confront
Morris's alliance of aestheticism and socialism, in *Demos*, he
showed no real understanding of it. This again constitutes an
ideological limitation. The oddest thing about all Gissing's novels
in the 1880's is that they postulate "art" as something entirely
unconscious of his own novel's existence, as though the novels
themselves were reports on the failure to produce true works of
art. What happens in *Workers in the Dawn* is in some ways
typical. Immediately after this, Mark and Arthur are presented as
living in their lodgings isolated from the other guests as though
to emphasise the purely theoretical nature of their commitment.

and Arthur then becomes involved with Carrie Mitchell—his relationship with the working class becomes personal as opposed to political. At this point it merely becomes a trap: Arthur's only way of making a marriage is to try to transform Carrie into a middle-class lady. Gissing's fictional talent is most in evidence at this point because it becomes as oppressive for the woman as for the man who is limited by her ignorance and turpitude. But it stresses the class nature of the ideological/cultural gap. Here at the very beginning the distance hinges on linguistic abuse. As Arthur finds his art only possible within a class-structured society in which a portion of the created wealth can liberate a section of the community from the toil that dehumanises the masses, so he can only create his woman as a sexual object by giving her the forms of that section. Undoubtedly, the affair with Carrie carries the plot away from the issues of radical politics and artistic talent, characteristically transforms the problem of the proletariat into that of the *lumpenproletariat,* but at the same time it reveals something very crucial about Gissing's ideological situation.

It becomes clear that in order to account for the social position of art, even in this first, apparently positivist novel, Gissing has to mystify it into a form of wayward "creativity". When Arthur meets up with the philanthropic intellectual Helen Norman (who has found her salvation through a synthesis of Comte, Schopenhauer and a distinctly deradicalised Shelley), she chides him for ever thinking that his art can be trivial or useless:

> We who toil on from day to day doing our little best to lessen the sum of the world's misery are doing good work, it cannot be denied; but what is this compared with the labour of men of genius, labour the results of which stand as milestones on the highway of civilisation, each one marking a great and appreciable advance?

> (III, vii)

Art is thus granted a teleological autonomy which makes for a strict division between the intellectual proper whose role (significantly "toil") is to alleviate the misery of the world and the creative "genius" who "labours" to make milestones on the highway of civilisation. The distinction operates both within the

54

middle class and the working class: a transcendent division between those who, like Helen and Arthur's radical mentor, Will
Noble, are born for action, and those who are "gifted . . . with
genius". The special laws for the genius are underwritten by the
mystified elevation of art itself. We have little sense of what
Arthur's paintings are like, but in another solemn dialogue with
Helen, he defines its emotional place:

> I know scarcely anything of the life which is raised above sordid
> cares and miseries, except from what I have read in books and
> imagined in my too frequent day-dreams; yet no sooner do I
> take up a pencil than I seem to taste all the delights of a higher
> and nobler existence, where the only food which is yearned after
> is that of the mind and the heart, and where the joys and
> sorrows are deeper and purer than those of the everyday world.
> (III, ix)

There is nothing in later Gissing to suppose that he ever departs
from this conception of art as the product of non-active genius
creating a nobler existence except, of course, his whole practice
as a novelist. "Noble" is a keyword in Gissing, and I do not think
it irrelevant that his conception of the hierarchical difference between the active and the creative man resembles a major tenet
of Yeats's aesthetic (as, of course, does the linking of the world
of art with the world of dream) It is, like Yeats's, a more or
less romantic commonplace, but the vocabulary is significantly
social. The toiler and the genius, the notion of a nobler existence
which is *higher* than his own, where joys and sorrows are *purer*
—such terms could apply as well to the contrast of social worlds,
to a class difference. In *Workers in the Dawn* this is obscured
by the veils of idealism and undigested theory, but it is con-
fusedly there in the contrast between Helen who is the subject
of artistic inspiration and Carrie who is a limitation. What further
confirms this class conception of the world of art is the way in
which Bohemianism is described, in the novel, simply as a phase
that refined sensibilities are likely to go through, but which has
no standing as an alternative world. As for Yeats, for Gissing,
the world of art has to be identified with a specific class structure.
The difference is that Gissing could never delude himself into
thinking that he was inside that world: it remains an aspiration,

a locked door which can only be recollected through one's acquired learning, or through a sublimation of class difference into manners. Above all, it generates the key notion of exile. A number of consequences flow from this. In the first place, since Gissing's conception of art does not include his own practice (in his novels, joys and sorrows are neither pure nor deep), his novels have to remain instrumental: in one sense they cannot be works of art, they can only be registers of art's impossibility, records of the failure of gifted talents held in exile. Secondly, Gissing settles to a very strange kind of conservatism. *Demos*, which is his most complete engagement with the problem of art and radicalism, at once mocks the delusory attempts of the Morris-like intellectual to unify a conception of beauty with an opposition to the class hierarchy, but at the same time satirises precisely that class which excludes the artist, by its philistinism, from the place where he can live the higher existence he is gifted to create. Finally, and more importantly, it leads him to expose the real conditions of intellectual life, which are only superficially explicable in terms of Poggioli's distinction, only explicable, that is, as an abstraction. For, essentially, the lives both of the intelligentsia and the intellectual élite are products of their social functionality, and art, or beauty, this higher existence which is untainted with mundane conditions, is ultimately dependent on a precise ordering of those conditions. *Isabel Clarendon*, for all its laborious snobbery, seems to me to reflect this precisely. Isabel herself, who is cultivated as an image superior to the world in which she exists, is precisely unable to be taken from the conditions of that world because her entry into it has created her what she is. Gissing is one of the most reactionary writers I know, and it is precisely because he is so reactionary that he cannot, without the privilege that would make "labour" supererogatory, create works of art in his sense, that he creates fictions which completely expose both the myth of creativity itself, and the class structure on which such myths depend. *Born in Exile* is the novel in which these contradictions are most effectively worked out, not specifically as the history of artistic aspiration, but more inclusively as the career of the intellectual seeking a functionality his very learning derides.

3

I want to stress the concept of a career because although there is much debate of ideological issues in all of Gissing's novels, it is always linked to the actual location of his protagonists in history because they all belong, more or less, to what Gramsci calls "the professional category of the intellectuals" (even Luckworth Crewe the advertising agent in *In the Year of the Jubilee* falls into this category). And I think this is something rare in English fiction. Of course, strictly speaking, there are no non-intellectuals, since everybody thinks, but, as Gramsci says, the term has meaning if we link it to an "immediate social function". Of course, there are plenty of intellectuals in this specific sense in English fiction too—priests, academics, writers—but, in the major instances at least, their position in the social system is either very marginal (I think of Will Ladislaw in *Middlemarch* or Vernon Whitford in *The Egoist*) or given (Casaubon and the long line of priests), or made the subject of social forces which by-pass the need of an intellectual career (Pip in *Great Expectations*, Daniel Deronda). Even when the question is raised as a major focus of fictional exposure, it tends to be within the specific framework of an established class function: Nickleby is a teacher, Carker a manager, Lydgate a doctor, and Meredith's Beauchamp a politician. Gissing, however, raises the question of the social role of a particular talent and training in *Born in Exile*, and asks it not of a free-wheeling individual but of an individual defined as the member of a group—the category of intellectuals. In fact, this gives the novel a strangely European quality, places it in line with *Le Rouge et Le Noir*, *Fathers and Sons* and *The Devils*.

The most useful approach to the novel is, as I have already implied, through the writings of Gramsci. For Gramsci makes clear that the word "intellectual" does not apply to an intrinsic characteristic (all men are intellectuals insofar as they think) but to the social function of an identifiable group which performs a wide range of tasks in the productive system:

> Every social group, coming into existence on the original terrain of an essential function in the world of economic production, creates together with itself, organically, one or more strata of

intellectuals which give it homogeneity and an awareness of its own function not only in the economic but also in the social and political fields.

(*Prison Notebooks*, p. 5)

Thus the arrival of capitalists requires various specialists who organise technology, the legal system, culture, etc. They are guardians of the dominant group's "hegemony"—that is, they ensure that it has power not only over production but over the whole social apparatus. He makes a distinction here between "state coercive power" (the law, etc.) and, a more important function, the power which is achieved by "spontaneous" consent of the masses to the general direction imposed on social life by the dominant fundamental group. Teachers, journalists, and politicians, for example, are organic intellectuals who win and retain this consent through particular forms of communication. Hence the need for an education system whose form will support the mode of production.

This is complicated, however, because there is an historic continuity in intellectual life which cuts across the specific historical needs of a particular mode of production. Every "essential social group" has to create its own intellectuals, but also finds a category of intellectuals created by preceding social structures and given coherence not by its organic function but by historical continuity, an *esprit de corps*. Gramsci terms this category that of the "traditional" intellectuals as opposed to the organic intellectuals created specifically for the tasks required by the dominant group. Traditional intellectuals seem to be autonomous, and one of the most important functions of hegemony is to conquer them "ideologically". It achieves this more efficiently insofar as it is able to create its own organic intellectuals. Capitalism is dominated by a class which "poses itself as an organism in continuous movement, capable of absorbing the entire society, assimilating it to its own cultural and economic level" (p. 260), and therefore sets up a continuous expansion of intellectual functions, attempting both to broaden the individual through education and to specialise him for the function he is to perform. State education becomes a necessity under capitalism in order to create a broad democratic base for the selection of middle and higher intellectual functionaries. The traditional intellectual with his

sense of continuity is vital both for the broadening (the dissemin-
ation of a determined level of "autonomous" culture) and the
specialisation (the preservation of an élite by which the higher
intellectual functions may be given a normative characteristic).

Because it was the first industrial capitalist society, England
has a particular feature which marks it off from other states.
Although the new dominant group had to create its own organic
intellectuals, for a long time it allowed the land-owning aristocracy to retain its politico-intellectual supremacy and remain the
main source of traditional intellectuals. Of course, this began to
change after the clashes between the aristocracy and the bourgeoisie over, for example, the Reform Acts and the Corn Laws. But
although this compelled the elaboration of new, bourgeois traditional intellectuals, the aristocratic hegemony remained potent at
least on an ideological level: the state education apparatus mim-
icked the aristocratic apparatus, the grammar school mimicking
the public school, the new universities mimicking Oxbridge. By the
end of the nineteenth century, we have a very complex situation
—an expanding group of traditional intellectuals loyal to an
aristocratic culture but increasingly deserted by the artistocracy
itself (the tension is evident in Arnold's assault on the barbarians,
and in the plethora of mediaeval idylls which yearned for an
artistocracy which would do more than collect and spend rents).
Of course, there is also a strong new middle-class culture too—
positive science, liberalism, the novel are the most obvious signs
of this. But "culture" strongly tends until very late to be identified
with Oxbridge and the Country House (W. H. Mallock's satire,
The New Republic, is a good index of this). Gissing's novel grows
out of the fraught anomalies of this situation: the traditional
intellectual, educated by capitalist money, conscious of bourgeois science thrust into a world whose ideology is still "aristocratic"—the more so as the bourgeoisie itself becomes more
and more populated with *rentiers* whose lifestyle necessarily resembles that of the "gentry", and whose privilege depends not on
the "free' thought of bourgeois ideology but on the mystification
of the masses by culture and religion.

Born in Exile is Gissing's most complete fiction of the "modern
mind" and by this I mean two things. First it is an epistemological adventure, an encounter with ideas and values that con-

stitute the morphology of the intellectual landscape: no other book of Gissing's has a plot so highly motivated by debate and a texture so dominated by literary allusion. But secondly, it is precisely characteristic of Gissing that this adventure should be seen also as a career: Peak's intellectual emancipation, his encounter, as it were, with the changing *esprit de corps* of the traditional intellectual is located as a problem of social mobility, of the organicism of that emancipation. This means that the epistemological ordeal is defined not merely as an engagement with ideas but as an ideological situation, a process of self-definition by the given terms of the institutions of ideological co-ercion—most notably education and marriage (or more accurately the family, since Peak's basic movement is from his own biological family into the Warricombe family, which Gissing is concerned to establish as an operative social group). These two levels, that of the "theme" of modernism and that of the "plot" of social mobility, work dialectically in relation to one another—that is to say, they work in contradiction on the one hand, since for Peak his intellectual enlightenment has to be hidden in the interests of his social integration, and in mutual reinforcement on the other, since it is the scientific spirit that enables Peak to perceive his own determinations and to play a game that will exploit them to the full (equally, it is the limitation of his knowledge that makes him play a game that is self defeating). This interaction of levels, its siting within the ideological systems of education and the family makes the novel strictly comparable with *Jude the Obscure* with this difference—that *Born in Exile* is *Jude* in reverse. For Jude too is born in exile and aspires towards an integration through culture. But Jude's journey is through and beyond theology towards knowledge as it is through and beyond marriage towards the "free" family that he creates with Sue. In other words it is a dislocating war upon the hegemony. Whereas Peak's is a journey back from science to theology, back from the freedom of Bohemian opposition towards the family and his death in exile, is not like Jude's a protest against an oppressive system but simply a record of the failure to achieve integration. Both Jude and Peak fight their intellectual battles as a class war, but they fight it in different directions.

The ideological project of the novel is made explicit when

Peak is trying to gain Sidwell Warricombe's sympathy with a calculated partial sincerity:

> When you first saw me I was a gawky schoolboy, learning to use my brains, and knowing already that life had nothing to offer me but a false position. Whether I remained with my kith and kin, or turned my back upon them in the hope of finding my equals, I was condemned to a life of miserable incompleteness. I was born in exile. It took a long time before I had taught myself how to move and speak like one of the class to which I belonged by right of intellect. I was living alone in London, in mean lodging houses. But the day came when I felt more confidence in myself. I had saved money, and foresaw that in a year or two I should be able to carry out a plan, make one serious attempt to win a position among educated people.
>
> (V, ii)

What is central here is the inevitability of "false position". It occurs because what dominates Peak's mind is a concept of class, and although this is ideologically modified, it is not in such a way that the class structure is challenged. On the contrary it is almost mystically reinforced since it is possible to belong to it by "right of intellect". It is a case, within a very mundane context, of the romance motif of the misplaced royal child. We note too how Peak instinctively sees his education as one of learning "how to move and speak" like the members of his lost class. The idea of social mobility is confined to the level of appearances. The whole idea comes to look like an anachronistic revival of the nature/ nurture debate that we find in Spenser and Shakespeare. Moreover, the word "class" is defined statically—here as "educated people" —as a group whose members possess certain attributes, rather than as a group which performs a certain function in the mode of production. We can see that Gissing's explicit grasp of class relations is highly mystified. Class is all important in Gissing, but not because it explains the way in which society works, but because it offers an institutionalised manifestation of a given individuation. Class is identical with both rank and race. Nevertheless if it is mystified as an object of aspiration (the right class is a form of Utopia) it is also in itself a secularising agency. The great good place is a real set of material conditions, and the only way to achieve those conditions is to find a function that will

61

lead one to it. The situation may resemble romance, but there are no romance solutions. Precisely because the concept of class is idealised in this way, Gissing is fictionally able to expose the real nature of its determinations. If you reductively describe the plot of *Born in Exile* as the story of Peak's sacrifice of his intellectual integrity for the sake of social integration, you miss the whole force of the fiction which this project sets in motion.

The bulk of the novel takes place between 1884 and 1886, and this is important because it is in precisely those years that Gissing evolves as a novelist trying to find an organic intellectual function. At the start of that period, he writes *Mrs. Grundy's Enemies* and *The Unclassed* which situate him as a novelist of Bohemian opposition (the former novel is lost but its title and the fact that both Bentley and Chatto were too scared to publish it gives us a fairly clear indication of what it was about).[3] In other words. they celebrate a class of intellectuals that preserve a critical integrity outside the hegemony. But what follows these is Gissing's flirtation with the Gaussens, and *Isabel Clarendon* and *Demos*, both of which celebrate culture as a class domain threatened by democratic emancipation. So that we move from a Bohemian commitment to an almost *arriviste* attempt to achieve integration (I have dealt with the reception of *Demos* in an earlier article and what is evident is the widespread welcome of its flagrant misrepresentations).[4] Peak may be in many ways identified with his creator, but it is only within a historical perspective, a perspective that includes a decisive assessment—not that Peak is seen with much irony (it is the failure of the novel that at the point at which he ought to be ironised, when Peak's choice of a role opposed to his intellectual integrity is placed in the context of the bohemian world he has rejected, he is virtually absent from the book), but the actual context of his development is revealed with a fictional density that transforms the project into a visible image thus opening the novel up to our view. Peak, that is, becomes a *case*.

I think it is worth tracing the first part of his history in some detail in order to show this density. The first part of the novel forms a prelude which sets up certain motifs that play through the novel. The most obvious of these is the linked problematic of intellectual emancipation and social mobility. Beginning as it does with the awarding of prizes, the world of intellectual attainment is instantly linked with the ritual of social selection and the nature of patronage. Whitelaw College is the product of raw capitalism, but the bestower of science and culture, the breeder of the ideological supremacy which capitalism has to conquer to survive. So that it is notably ironic that Peak should feel it necessary to leave because his uncle determines to open a pie shop. What is most significant is that the question of mobility should be posed in the terminology of Social Darwinism:

> Happily he is of the robust sex; he can hit out right and left, and make standing room. We have armed him with serviceable weapons, and now he must use them against the enemy—that is to say, against all mankind, who will quickly enough deprive him of sustenance if he fail in the conflict . . . He has been born and he must eat. By what licensed channel may he procure the necessary viands?
>
> (I, ii)

The social Darwinian context (the concept of the survival of the fittest) pervades the book. Peak's colleague, Earwacker, for example, is "naturally marked for survival among the fittest" (II, i). Peak himself finds that the landscape in which the Warricombes live offers "security from the struggle of life" (II, iii) and at the end of the novel, Sidwell tells him that "You have been trying to adapt yourself . . . to a world for which you are by nature unfitted" (VI, iv). This kind of vocabulary is not uncommon in Gissing but it has a special function here because it builds a bridge between the social reality and the intellectual enlightenment. For, of course, Job Whitelaw's college not only creates social mobility, it also licenses (if reluctantly) the science which exposes the ideology of the social fabric, for if it does not teach Peak "the advanced guard of modern thought" it puts him in touch with and stimulates him to study "the science that had completely broken with tradition" (I, ii). His choice of an alternative to the B.A. is significantly the School of Mines for "on every hand, the future was with the students of the law of matter" (I, iv). Social Darwinism, at least as it is manifested in the work of Herbert Spencer whose most overtly ideological essay, *Man Versus the State* was published in the years in which this novel is set, is an obvious vindication of straightforward militant capitalism, but it has its ironic repercussions. For capitalism is only so starkly "naturalistic" in the phase in which it has not yet accomplished the control over the social apparati of oppression. Once it has conquered society it becomes the master also of the social machinery which relies on mystification and codes of behaviour to exact the subjection of its members. Peak's hypocrisy is born on the margins of this discrepancy: he is compelled to become a self-made man in a world in which self-making is no longer respectable. But more immediately, it also means that the very science which capitalism makes possible, creates on its margins a class which is critical of its ideology. When Sidwell accuses Peak of trying to adapt to a world to which he is unfitted, she is contrasting an "old world" with a new to which by nature he belongs. The middle sections of the novel are not concerned with a unilateral assault by the exile on the fortress of privilege, but with his movement from the new world to the old.

The second and third parts of the novel seem to me to constitute some of the best of Gissing's writing: each part has for its structure a movement away from the new world which is established in the opening section to the singling out of Peak and his dilemma and from this to his interaction with the Warricombe family which leads to a developed analysis of his epistemological situation. At the same time there is an incremental development from one section to the other. The first chapter of Part II establishes a social group around John Earwacker the radical journalist who is struggling to preserve his integrity against guttersnipe radicalism, and raises the issues of knowledge and marriage as questions of debate, while the opening chapter of Part III focusses on the same group and the same issues but now both places Peak in confrontation with the group and dramatises the debated issues of the first section so that Peak's personal predicament is given a context, notably through the sexual naïveté of Malkin's theory of the *école des femmes* and Moxey's absurd cult of Petrarchan love. II, ii begins with Peak alone in London and traces the motivation of his rejecting the values of the liberal world which is tenderly celebrated in the first chapter; III, ii again has him alone, this time in Exeter, rationalising both to himself and to another, as he had done in the previous section, both religious compromise and what Earwacker is later to call Peak's "preposterous sexual spectacles". In the earlier section however, he talks to Earwacker in whom he confides both about religion and sex, whereas as in this later chapter, he talks to Martin Warricombe, on whom he is practising hypocrisy, about religion alone and the sexuality is internalised. II, iii has Peak being assimilated into the Warricombe circle unconsciously and naturally, while III, iii has him being thought about and discussed by members of the family as a figure to be reckoned with. And the fourth chapter of each section records different phases of the Stendhalian game: the movement from a "wasted integrity" to the perception of a field of conquest in the first, and the movement from that field as motivation (the visionary transport of love which defies rational enquiry) to the momentary perception that the "hypocritic comedy" might be superfluous in the second. These parallels and increments of structure represent the whole strategy of the novel, the movement from a shared theoretical position (the new world) to the concrete actuality of making it work within the confines of the old. We witness as we move between the two sections the progressive individuation of Peak as he begins to fight as a personal battle the contradictions inherent in the world and its opposing groups defined in the first section. But this has a further purpose. Gissing keeps several different issues going throughout the novel: an ideological debate about religion which seems always to end up entailing a debate about sex, since intellectual emancipation leaves male sexual egoism unaccounted for (Peak is loud in his contempt for emancipated women) and sexual desire is a second persistent level not merely for Peak but also for Moxey, Malkin and Buckland Warricombe. But sexual desire is also linked, through Peak's isolation and sense of deprivation with social aspiration. Ideology, sex and class thus become concentrated in Peak's individuation. Knowledge and social status pose themselves to him as radically opposed forces.

Three points need to be stressed about the realisation of this structure. First, that the process by which Peak projects himself from the potential new world of intellectual emancipation into an unavailable old world of the middle-class provincial family is *placed* not in terms of conventional morality but as a naïveté. Second, that this authorial placing does not undermine Peak's ordeal because it is realised in detail as an epistemological ordeal

—in other words, if Peak plays a self-defeating game it derives from a process of awareness that makes it necessary. And finally, that the novel does not resolve itself into the contradictory state that these two statements may seem to imply because Gissing affirms the hegemonic power of the world which Peak aspires to against the rational supremacy of the values he rejects. In other words it offers itself to the new member of the traditional intellectuals, as a field to be conquered but that itself is part of the conquest it practises.

The sense of naïveté offers itself from the beginning as authorial comment. The opening of I, iii makes it clear that Peak's "militant egoism" is repressed by a "coward delicacy" and that the co-existence of the two is self-destructive. Throughout the novel, Gissing draws ironic attention to the lapses in his consistency, as for example when he plans to marry on the basis of hypocritical professions and later reveal his agnosticism: "the wife whom he imagined (his idealism in this matter was of a crudity which made the strangest contrast with his habits of thought on every other subject) would be ruled by her emotions . . ." (III, ii). Peak obviously underestimates both the Warricombes' tolerance and open-mindedness, and their capacity to see through the game he plays. Moreover, he sees too late that his own family is not as simply banal as he thinks, and that he has only cut himself off from them to increase his solitude and desolation. Above all, however, Peak's worst naïveté seems to be the one that Sidwell of all people points out to him—that he turns his back on a new world to fight for a place in an old world in which there is no place for him. Earwacker is a crucial figure in this context, for, as we have seen, he is marked out for survival and yet, unlike most of Gissing's survivors he has a real integrity. Around him, the Moxeys and Malkin form a social group which stands apart from both the drabness of the petty bourgeoisie and the cosy complacencies of the rentier class. I have compared the novel to *Le Rouge et Le Noir* but in this it is significantly different. When Julien goes to Besançon, he finds the mediocrity of provincial life repeated in a supposedly intellectual context: the inmates of the seminary are still basically concerned to get material security. The pressure is inevitably towards Paris. Peak however goes to London, lives in modest comfort and finds friends with whom he can share his ideas and values. He is clearly not, at the beginning of Part II, a victim of circumstances. This is further stressed in II, ii when Gissing describes his lodgings in Peckham Rye. Unusually, they are not oppressive but are very comfortable. Later, when his game is fraught with complexities, he is to look back to his London life with longing. I think Gissing wants us to remain very aware of this throughout the novel. Indeed the chief function of Part IV seems to be to assert the validity of this world and the possibility of the impact it can make, via Marcella Moxey and Sylvia Moorhouse on the mind of an intelligent girl like Sidwell. This seems to be given a bitterly ironic twist when Peak is liberated from his limited means by the love of Marcella. That is the world of his potential success, and finally of whatever real success he has. Right to the end, he has the opportunity to be free and to win Sidwell at the same time. If we read the novel in terms of a rational and liberal morality, we seem to be confronted not only with a character who is dishonest, but who is also a fool. If Peak glorifies himself as the lost prince, he projects himself as a Tartuffe, and Moliere's world is as remote from the 1880s as is Spenser's.

And yet somehow, Gissing clearly expects us to remain interested in Peak's dilemma, and I think he succeeds (it is not a question of sympathy or identity—Gissing cares too much about the existential nakedness of the situation he portrays to worry too much about the possessive sensibilities of his bourgeois readers). You cannot read a Gissing novel in terms of a liberal morality because there is always more going on than such an abstraction allows for. And what challenges that reading above all is announced most forcibly in II, ii as the question of membership. We have seen Peak as a member of his family and turning against that: we have seen him as a (prizewinning) member of Whitelaw college and feeling himself to be both socially and intellectually dismembered from that. Here in London, we see him in a context which essentially offers no membership since it is a group of "free" intellectuals. What is stressed at the opening of II, ii is both the freedom and the loneliness of his life in London:

For himself, he had earned daily bread, and something more; he had studied in desultory fashion; he had seen a good deal of

67

the British Isles and had visited Paris. The result of it all was gnawing discontent, intervals of furious revolt, periods of black despair.
He had achieved nothing, and he was alone.

Not a bad life—merely an empty one, without any sense of belonging. He feels a "tormenting attraction" to walk in the wealthy districts of London: "Why was not one of these doors open to him?" In Hyde Park he watches from the edge of "a gaping plebeian crowd" two ladies reposing in their carriage in "Olympian calm"—"they were his equals, those ladies . . . With such as they he should by right of nature associate". Later in the chapter, he visits Earwacker and defends religious dogmas on the grounds that "There's a vast police force in them" and as the talk drifts inevitably towards marriage (which entails membership in more than one sense), Peak states "I am a plebeian and I aim at marrying a lady", and defines "lady" as "a woman of the highest type our civilization can produce". Earwacker warns him not to look for her in society, but Peak knows what he is on about. The traditional intellectual is a product of civilisation, of the accumulated wealth that has emancipated man from the simple reproduction of immediate needs, and he is the product of the class appropriation of that wealth. When Peak first goes to Exeter, he sees the physical world of the Warricombes as one in which one can be secure from the struggle for existence. For Gissing, as we have seen, the value of labour is that it releases a section of the community from the necessity of labour. In *Born in Exile* he inserts between the plebeian crowd and the Olympian ladies a margin in which the life of the mind can attain a kind of freedom. But it is a margin of emptiness, of being on the edge. Ironically, the life of the mind can only be pursued with the help of a police force of dogmas that keep Olympia safe from pickpockets.

The following chapter (II, ii) realises the preparations of this. In Exeter, Peak meets the Warricombes and the process of integration begins. First, as on the edge of the gaping crowd, Peak *perceives* the family and its friends: "all this was matter of observation for Peak, who had learnt to exercise his decernment even whilst attending to the proprieties". From perception, he moves to self-consciousness, from seeing others, to seeing his reflection: "Peak, after each of his short remarks, made comparison of his tone and phraseology with those of the other speakers." He overcomes his misgivings, and then is able to perform a brilliant recapitulation of the sermon he half heard at the cathedral "under the marvelling regard of his conscious self . . . more eloquent, more subtle". From discernment to reflection to performance and through this to acceptance. Being asked to join the ride, "he was accepted by his peers, and could regard with tolerance even those ignoble orders of mankind amid whom he had so long dwelt unrecognised". The following chapter re-enacts this momentary process in larger terms—observing the "luxury of the rational kind" evident in Martin Warricombe's study, accepting "the rare repose" of Mrs Warricombe's platitudes, using a mirror to declare himself ready and recalling the London which offered him no social advancement, Peak is moved towards a declaration of intent to take up orders. "The field of possible conquest" observed and entered, he rejects the absolute of integrity: "he was essentially a negativist guided by the mere relations of phenomena". Relativism, which is at the core of the critical ideology of the anti-bourgeois intelligentsia at the end of the nineteenth century, may seem to have found a strange manifestation here, but it is what constitutes the ideological definition of Gissing's uniqueness. For in the relativism of hypocrisy, the "erotic madness" and the life of the mind find a strange reconciliation: the traditional intellectual organises himself. Ideologically Peak observes with "the sensibility of the proletarian" (II, ii) but he can reconcile himself to the Church to some extent because it offers a cause to "combat the proletarian challenges" (III, ii). It is a class war Peak is fighting, both a war on his exclusion from Olympia, and a war to keep Olympia as a place to aspire to. And this is firmly linked to the erotic madness. Earwacker has decided to do without women, Moxey and Malkin cultivate socially conditioned ideals which are mystified into literary types. Peak's ideal is embodied in a class type: he loves Sidwell because she is representative, the ultimate Olympian prize. Gissing puts Peak through a persistent ordeal of doubt and speculation, but it is one that is ultimately tied in to the social function, the "marketable value of brains". Peak, for all his naïveté, because of his perversity, because his sensibility remains proletarian as his ideology tries to find him a place among the consumers of surplus value, tests, exposes this marketable value.

For finally, what is affirmed is the strength of the hegemony on which he practises his "Napoleonic" (II, iv) assault. Earwacker, Moxey and Malkin have dependencies on sources outside their world, and Peak has only his gaping crowd. The Warricombes are much more decent than he takes them for, but they represent a closed and privileged world. Old Martin with his vacillating milk and water modernism, like his friend Lillywhite, is "representative of a Divinity characterised by a well bred tolerance" (III, iv). And even Sidwell, though she tolerates the new world, always remains outside it (and would be unlovable if she didn't). But above all there is Buckland, himself emancipated, hovering between the two worlds, but motivated by what is reiterated again and again as class prejudice against Peak to observe him with what his father calls a "secret police". Peak can't win because the class system is bigger than him. The possible mobility is clearly marked—Bruno Chilvers, the daft modernist clergyman is the image of success, the perfect organic intellectual. There is nothing self-pitying about *Born in Exile*: it explores with cold honesty the margin of intellectual freedom, and finds it a mere transition. In capitalism, the intellectual has a role to perform. Peak doesn't, like Jude, refuse to perform it, but he performs it badly and his ineptitude reveals the truth about that role. You may not need to join the church to become a member of the ruling class, but you do need to know your place.

NOTES

1 Poole, op, cit., p. 207.
2 Gramsci, *Prison Notebooks* (1971), p. 18.
3 Gettman, *A Victorian Publisher: A Study of the Bentley Papers* (1960), pp. 215–23. This gives a detailed account of Bentley's handling of the novel. Bentley seems to have tried to sell the novel to Chatto as late as 1887, for there is a letter from the latter dated 14 February rejecting it. As far as I know this is unpublished, and the copy I have seen is in the Chatto and Windus Letterbooks, vol. 19, no. 826.
4 See *Victorian Studies*, vol. XII, December 1968.

3

The Evolution of the
Gissing Novel

1

The space in which Gissing's novels can achieve their distinctness
—a space identifiable in terms both of literary history and ideological situation—is one in which an unmediated materiality
is reflected in the unrequited idealism of the post-Dickensian
emancipated intellectual producer. But Gissing doesn't have this
distinctness ready made. On the contrary, the reason that I have
begun by giving so much attention to late texts is because I
want to see where he arrives, in other words to define the terms
of a "Gissing" novel This clearly has its own history—there is
an evolution towards that distinctness from a confused and disturbed conformity. In fact, I think that it takes Gissing the whole
of the 'eighties to arrive at the point where he could write his
own novels. *The Nether World* (1889) seems to me to be the
first novel in which Gissing makes a break with what has gone
before, and even that is uncharacteristic since it deals with the
working class out of a kind of philanthropic aesthetic. It is when
he is able to apply the formal, non-Dickensian qualities of that
text to the concerns being elaborated clumsily in inherited forms
in *The Unclassed, Isabel Clarendon, A Life's Morning* and *The
Emancipated*, that is with the predicament of his own group, the
unorganic lower middle-class intellectual, that we get the first
complete Gissing novel.

At present we are looking not *at* texts so much as *in* them for
two things: a development and the premature appearance of the

71

constituents of that late sequence of novels which make Gissing unique. These constituents appear in the texts of the 'eighties along with others that have to be transformed or rejected to enable the creation of a "combative" realism which rejects the possibility of an organic link between individuality and totality, to replace it with the special privilege of marginality and emancipation. It moves away from panorama (inclusiveness) towards the limited totality of the group, and sites itself not in the city as the landscape of a totality, but in the named London which is the zoned space of a determined mobility, as an enclosure rather than as an agglomeration. These three constituents make for a distinctive kind of representativeness, a different form of displacement from that of the convex mirror, but they only come to be the determinant features of the text as Gissing writes his way out of the high Victorian novel. The texts of the 'eighties divide themselves broadly into three groups. First, in a group of its own, though growing out of *Workers in the Dawn*, and probably closely linked with the lost *Mrs. Grundy's Enemies*, is *The Unclassed* which initiates in theme and even in method the features of the mature work, though in such an unfocussed way that they are lost in the mists of a dissolving conventional structure. Then *A Life's Morning* and *Isabel Clarendon* pick up and elaborate, outside the site that has been discovered in *The Unclassed*, the double predicament of marginality and enlightenment in terms of dramatised class relations. Finally *Demos* (slightly), *Thyrza* and *The Nether World* establish the London that is to be the site of Gissing's fiction by portraying the "problematic" of working-class life. These groups follow one another in time so that it is accurate to talk of an evolution.

2

There were present thirteen pupils, the oldest of them turned fifteen, the youngest scarcely six. They appeared to be the daughters of respectable people, probably tradesmen in the neighbourhood. The school was in Lisson Grove, in the north west of London; a spot not to be pictured from its name by those ignorant of the locality; in point of fact a dingy street, with a mixture of shops and private houses. On the front door was a plate displaying Miss Rutherford's name—nothing more.

That lady herself was middle aged, grave at all times, kindly, and, be it added, fairly competent as things go in the world of school. The room was rather bare, but the good fire necessitated by the winter season was not wanting, and the plain boarding of the floor showed itself no stranger to scrubbings. A clock hanging on the wall ticked very loudly in the perfect stillness as the schoolmistress took her seat. (I)

Already in this first descriptive passage of Gissing's second novel, much of the characteristic mode is here. *The Unclassed* has opened with a trivial melodrama—one child has struck another with a slate for insulting her mother—and it is one that is to have major narrative consequences, but this paragraph contains it within a daily normality, "a strange disorder" in the "abode of decorum". Ida Starr is to be expelled not for striking Harriet Smales, but because Harriet's insult is true—Ida's mother is a prostitute. Not that it has to be true for Miss Rutherford to act, merely likely enough to damage the school's respectability. But this narrative follows our passage—Miss Rutherford's visit to Harriet's home, and her evasive letter to Mrs. Starr. It is these episodes that initiate the theme of the unclassed in the novel. At present, apparently paradoxically, Gissing is concerned to establish a class situation. And we are alerted to a pattern of contrasts. On the one hand, the location—a real place named with an explicit consciousness of its remoteness from the reader (those ignorant of the locality) and of the ironic disjunction between the idyllic name and the dingy actuality. This location is developed through the first four chapters into the sense of an area—the mixed array of streets just north of the Marylebone Road and to the West of Regent's Park. Miss Rutherford has sent a child to a doctor in Grove Street; she visits Mr. Smales at his shop in Boston Street ("a little *out of the way* thorough-fare"—my italics). Ida in the second chapter runs home to Milton Street where her mother lives in an "apartment" above a dress-maker, and in the fourth, Maud Enderby spends Christmas Eve in "one of a row of semi-detached houses standing in gardens" which we later learn is in South Bank, adjacent to Regent's Park. A range of places, from the dingy to the respectable, a range of accommodation, from apartment to semi, but all within a "neigh-bourhood", remote but actual, out of the way but in London,

73

described but non-descript. Gissing's London—not "the city" as a conceptualised response, as a totality, but an area, a limited and limiting location. Mobility is problematic—Ida's journey to her grandfather in Islington in Chapter II is like a trip abroad. There will be other areas—Kennington, Fulham, Chelsea—but all delimited spaces that have to be lived in or crossed. A mixture, too, this neighbourhood, but a mixture within strict boundaries.

And yet this dinginess is placed against an affirmed respectability. A school in Dickens would be either nightmare or idyll. Miss Rutherford's is neither. If the room is bare, it is warm, if the floorboards are uncarpeted, they are scrubbed. If Miss Rutherford is middle-aged and mediocre, she is also competent and kind. The dinginess of the street is contrasted with the apparent respectability within—the pupils are "daughters of respectable people", and the three girls whose lives are singled out for representation from the thirteen are within important limits confirmations of this appearance. Harriet is really the daughter of a chemist, Maud Enderby lives with a respectable and modestly well-off maiden aunt. And even Ida, though her mother lives a life beyond the pale, has had an upbringing "in no respect inferior to that she would have received in the home of the average London artisan or small tradesman" (III). The place, the class are specific, yet the novel is to be about displacement and the "unclassed". Again this passage, with its mixture foreshadows this possibility. Miss Rutherford is kind—she does not want to expel Ida, but knows that the "irreproachable character" of her school demands it: "She sincerely regretted the step she must take, and to which she would not have felt driven by any ill-placed prudery of her own." The pupils *appear* to be the daughters of respectable people—that is what is demanded. But in the neighbourhood of Lisson Grove, such appearances are frail and under threat of exposure. And this is not only true of Ida, it is true also of Harriet and Maud. Chapters II and IV, "Mother and Child" and "Christmas in Two Homes" make this clear. Ida and her mother are not represented as mother and child at all but as two children:

> The one a child lost on weary woeful ways, knowing, yet untaught by, the misery of desolation; the other a child still standing upon the misty threshold of unknown lands, looking around

for guidance, yet already half feeling that the sole guide and comforter was within. (II)

Christmas in the two homes of Harriet and Maud is obviously a contrast with Ida's desolation, just as obviously they contrast with one another. Yet what is striking is what pulls them together. For Harriet literally has no mother, and her father has effectively given up the struggle for existence: "Mr. Smales himself was always depressed in mind and ailing in body. Life had proved too much for him; the burden of recurring daylight was beyond his strength" (IV). He is soon to die, and Harriet to be sent to an aunt in Colchester to learn the stationery trade. When she next appears in the novel, she is working in the Grays Inn Road, looked after only by Mr. Smales' nephew, the half Italian Julian, himself an orphan closed in on a private world of imagination. Maud goes to her puritanical aunt who on Christmas Eve teaches her that the world only exists to be renounced. Later we learn that her father has drifted into embezzlement and her mother gone mad. The family is so important and so potentially defective in this area of society. Miss Rutherford runs a decent school, but its availability depends on economic viability and moral respectability. That is also what insertion depends on. But, because it is a fringe area, neither capitalist nor proletarian, it is also continually beckoning its members towards the edge of the social world, to make of them outsiders who are trapped within the domain that expels them.

The novel never quite lives up to this opening, and I have dwelt on it because it seems to me to look forward to the mature Gissing who can work out such motifs fictionally. Much of what is latent here can only be elaborated through the introduction of a new character who theorises these contradictions. But even Waymark who is so much of an exponent character is caught in the predicament of the unclassed. Like the three girls, he has a class. Son of a businessman become a schoolteacher, his unclassed nature is a kind of surplus that his place does not take account of. But the way in which he announces himself is significant. The first we hear of him is through a personal advertisement in the columns of a newspaper:

"Wanted, human companionship." He announces himself

75

"student of ancient and modern literatures, a free-thinker in religion, a lover of art in all its forms, a hater of conventionalism." It ought to be matter for comedy, but it isn't because it is a sign of urban isolation. Again place is real and important: Julian Casti has to go from Oxford Street to Kennington to find this "O.W." who is in need of companionship. The paid-for announcement, a shooting in the dark across the functional zones of the city. Once Waymark comes into the novel, the issues foreshadowed in the opening chapters become ideologically explicit. For Waymark the artist has accomplished a theoretical disengagement: "I was bent on an intellectual life forsooth; couldn't see that the natural order of things was to make money first and be intellectual afterwards" (VII). His "combative nature" can be translated into a polemical egotism which seeks a new form of satire against "the vile restraints of Philistine surroundings" (VI). Unlike Casti, he can link the passion for art with the hatred of society not by creating an alternative world, but by a modernism which transmutes his own "suffering" into art. He can translate Maud's religiosity into a rationalised Schopenhauerian position. But this ideological gloss is less important than what Waymark is shown to be, the limitations of his disengagement which finally make his commitment to art unimportant: the actual publication of the novel he writes is passed over with a wry comment about its reception, and at the end of the novel, we are told that "his enthusiasm for art was falling away" (XXXIII). It leads nowhere, because it is merely a transitional defence against the potential emptiness of his life. The fictional significance of Waymark is not in what he says of himself in the advertisement, but the medium through which he says it. It is a measure of his effectivity, a measure of the narrow area of freedom in which he is allowed to realise himself—what Hardy's Sue Bridehead is later to call a "theoretic unconventionality" whose practice is ultimately entirely in the hands of Ida.

Ida is often taken to be a glib piece of idealism, but that is only true if we take the novel as a collection of separate characters, and not as a group defined by its unclassed nature which has limited possibilities of movement acted out by its members who only meet through contingencies that are determined for them. What is important is that Waymark, by the time he arrives on the scene has already reached a point of theoretical disengagement (it is evident, for example, in his description of his radical phase as being a false identification with the working class) whereas we see Ida at the end of her childhood confronted with a choice between accepting the "fatherhood" of her rack-renting grandfather or living entirely alone, and projecting herself consciously into the unprotected struggle ("He's *not* my father . . . my father is dead; and now mother's dead, and I'm alone"). We do not see her again until Waymark meets her, and it is as a function of a relationship between these two most articulate members of the group that she exists in the novel. First we must attend to the way they meet. Waymark in an earlier chapter has said farewell to Casti late at night with the remark "Oh, it is my hour for walking . . . London streets at night are my element" (VII). It is, of course, a remark that fits with the general pose of the modern aesthete (the right context would be that analysed in Benjamin's essay on the *flaneur*).[1] Later, after he has been to see Maud Enderby whom he has protected from the insults of her employer and found her an ideal woman breathing in "the intellectual atmosphere of my own creation" (XI), he goes to the theatre and wanders from the Strand into Pall Mall. Here he gives a sovereign to a prostitute who cannot pay her cab fare and this act of generosity makes Ida speak to him. She then uses him to get away from a pursuer, treats him to supper and takes him back to her room in Temple Bar ("I should be ill if I had to live in one of those long, dismal streets, where the houses are all the same shape, and costermongers go bawling about all day long. I suppose you live in a place like that"). What starts with Waymark being patronising ("The life you have chosen brings its inevitable consequences" . . . "How do you know that I had any choice in the matter?") ends with him admiring and for once doing less of the talking. The location is important: the hustle of the city streets with its random contingencies is London, but only part of Gissing's London. Mostly, the novel is based on areas with contained social structures which hold even the unclassed within them—the West End is a specific location within the city, not the city itself. Moreover, Waymark wanders there out of aesthetic curiosity: Ida lives and works there. A precise structure of relationships is being worked out at this point.

77

Waymark dominates Casti, and he is to dominate Maud whose emancipation he presides over with his superior theoretic detachment. But he has also resigned from his post as a teacher and is to become Abraham Woodstock's rent-collector. Ida is where she is because she has refused Woodstock's patronage. Waymark declares himself above moral judgments, Ida is indifferent to her judgments on her own life. The whole relationship is summarised by her remark about living in Temple Bar: she lives where Waymark likes to let his imagination roam. She acts out his theoretic unconventionality. Later she tells him that she has chosen prostitution because she has rejected the "slavery" of being a sempstress, "because sewing is a woman's natural slavery" (XVII). She bursts into the novel as a challenge to the frail community of intellectual blood-brothers Waymark has been finding up to this point:

> The novel circumstances of the past week had almost driven from his mind all thought of Maud Enderby. He regretted having asked and obtained permission to write to her. She seemed so remote from him, their meeting so long past. What could there be in common between himself and that dim quiet little girl; who had excited his sympathy merely because her pretty face was made sad by the same torments which had afflicted him? He needed some strong vehement, original nature, such as Ida Starr's. (XIV)

Of course, Gissing is portraying a very untypical prostitute: Ida is not "a common girl", but her decision, her acting out of the unconventionality, is a convincing matter of integrity. There is nothing self-indulgent about it: Waymark is outstripped by Ida —he continually retreats into doubt, contempt and a kind of betrayal with Maud. The problem which Gissing cannot solve is how to elaborate the contingency into relationship.

The problem is deeply related both to the nature of class in the novel and to the specific form of Gissing's London. The first time Ida and Waymark go out together is on an excursion to Richmond. For the first time he sees Ida without make-up and finds her paler but still healthy. As they move from the city the isolation it generates begins to fall away: "the troubles of passion, the miseries of self-consciousness, the strain of mutual

78

observation fell from them as the city dropped behind; they were once more creatures for whom the external world alone had reality" (XV). It promises a different possibility of life from the urban world. But only as an excursion. Ida is accompanied by her friend, Sally, and on the way, they meet two of Waymark's former schoolteaching colleagues, one of whom falls in love with Sally, who decides to live a better life, as he decides to throw off the slavery of schoolteaching. They will make a relationship, found a new life as small shopkeepers in Peckham Rye. The park as nature, the suburb as the domain of the new life, shopkeeping as independence—these are all that are offered as concrete possibilities, and Sally and Mr. O'Gree are of course decent and comic, rustic innocents who can find a kind of Dickensian simplicity. Obviously, for Waymark and Ida to make a relationship, Ida's life will have to change too, and this is symbolically signified when she bathes naked at midnight, and later becomes a laundress in Fulham. The trouble is that inevitably in washing away the uncleanness of her former life, she washes away her original nature too. She is committed to the long streets and woman's natural slavery. After this, the novel retreats into a sequence of machinations: Harriet trapping Ida into being accused of theft; Waymark being beaten up in Litany Lane so that her martyrdom and his doubts become sublimated into a romantic confrontation. Woodstock is killed and Maud's family disgraced so that all the commitments and rejections of the first part become irrelevant. But what else is there in the city of the unclassed? How, except by compromise or romance, can the West End, the Park and the Suburb release those caught in the residential areas on which those zones of contingency, freedom and newness depend? Equally, what more honest profession is there for the intellectual than that of rent-collector, and for the free woman than prostitution?

In this novel, Gissing poses unanswerable questions and tries to answer them with an ending which is part of the stock-in-trade of the romantic novelist. This is the more ironic since Ida has already said that in real life endings are so commonplace. But the failure of the novel is identical with its significance. The concept of the unclassed is a condition of the deep structure of Gissing's specific effectivity. We should make a distinction here between unclassed and declassed, now that we have seen the way in which the fictional world of Gissing structures itself. Declassment is virtually a condition of the classic realist novel: the protagonist, in order that he may become a convex mirror, has to be displaced from a given world and sent on a journey to another—as Tom Jones is expelled from Paradise Hall, or Fanny Price moved from Portsmouth to Mansfield or Pip taken out of the smithy. But the condition of being unclassed is not exactly to be displaced, it is to be in a place that has no bearing on a potential function. It grants the protagonist no privilege, no convexity. Gissing's characters can only at best theoretically see beyond the horizon of their location. And that is why his novels, for all that they deal with characters on the fringe of society, characters caught in class mobility, never really single out a "protagonist"—the knowledge can only be shared, as the city which is the domain of this knowledge is necessarily zoned. So the condition of being unclassed becomes too general—it is only by the focussing of the unclassed nature on a topic, an issue, that the contingencies which make for narrative can be built. In this novel, characters are brought together by the synoptic eye of the novelist. What Gissing will evolve towards is a social zoning, people occupying the same terrain. But meanwhile we can see what he is moving towards—the social condition of being placed in an empty space where all that has meaning is a struggle for existence. And we can see too how he arrives at that—through the creation of his own London, a London named and mapped, where even the openings are fenced off, like the parks and the suburbs. But it will take Gissing a long time to achieve that focus. First, he has to work out the loneliness as a function of displacement, and at the same time, in a separate order of fictions, work out the place that his London is as a set of class relations. We see, in *The Unclassed*, the fundamental motif, naked and untransformed, as an ideology rather than as a fiction, hopelessly broken against its own rational consequence which can have no concrete elaboration. And we see a domain, the urbanised city, a city which has grown beyond its productive and commercial functions, but still open to reform (so that if you can't deny the long streets, you can do something about the slums). It is the coalescence of the motif and the domain that is the sign of Gissing's uniqueness.

3

The Unclassed was published in the summer of 1884. After a short break, Gissing embarked on a remarkably productive period lasting eighteen months during which he produced three novels, *Isabel Clarendon* (written between October 1884 and March 1885,) *A Life's Morning* (August to October 1885) and *Demos* (November 1880 to early March 1886). The next two novels, *Thyrza* and *The Nether World*, took more than two years to produce. None of these three are very successful, but they show Gissing trying to develop a focus for the ideological polemic of *The Unclassed*. It is very significant that all three contain within them a preoccupation with the nature and status of art. *Isabel Clarendon* is full of undigested statements about the novel and the relationship of artistic production to the social structure. *A Life's Morning* also has direct authorial comments on its own form, and *Demos* has as one of its central figures a poet committed to socialism, as well as a newly rich working-class girl who finds nothing better to do than read novels. Two kinds of comment are especially revealing. One is about the possibilities of writing accurate fiction which is seen most startlingly in a sudden authorial outburst in the middle of an account of the mother of the heroine of *A Life's Morning*: "After the birth of her first child, Emily, her moral nature showed an unaccountable weakening; the origin was no doubt physical, but in story-telling we dwell very much on the surface of things; it is not permitted us to describe human nature too accurately" (V). The implication that to portray the physiological reality of a character's make-up is to go below the surface is a rare direct allegiance to the French naturalists, but it is a comment coherent with the remarks about Gabriel's painting in *Isabel Clarendon*, a straining against the limitations of treatment and subject felt by the novelist who wishes to write stories that will not match the conventions of story-telling (there is a characteristic moment later when one of the more radical characters says "We are not living in a novel; there are no such things as mysteries which last a lifetime" [XVII] —and that to a large extent summarises the contradictory tension within the fiction of the 'eighties in general, between the function of the novel as wet nurse of ideology, and its function as demystifying mirror). On the other hand, the second kind of comment stresses the need for aesthetic distance: thus Thomas Meres in *Isabel Clarendon* tells Ada Warren that her novel is "for a work of art . . . too subjective. It reads too much like a personal experience which the writer is not far enough away from to describe with regard to artistic proportion . . . You have got outside of the subject, and looked at it all round" (II, vi), and he asks her to write a story which is completely imaginary. It ties in with Kingcote's comment that for fiction "I am vastly too subjective" (II, viii). Both the fact that the novels contain these reflexive comments and the nature of the comments themselves suggest that the productivity of this period results from an attempt to find a mode of fiction which enables Gissing to achieve what Hardy is later to call "candour in fiction", a candour which has to proceed from what Waymark has termed the polemical egoism of the artistic temperament, and at the same time to distance that candour in a form that will accede to lifelong mysteries. A specific ideology, in other words, that will be an authentic reflection.

What Kingcote says about himself, however, is true of the novel in which he exists. Its rather frail story is very much a peg on which to hang polemical essays that state Gissing's pessimism and conservatism. Not that it fails because it is a novel of ideas. Rather it is because the ideas which Kingcote brings to the novel are never sufficiently exposed to the world they encounter. Potentially, as a number of critics have noted, it is a great step forward for Gissing, for instead of the polemical egoism existing on the sidelines as an undigested gloss, it is elaborated not merely as polemic but as the definition of a "temperament". Consider, for example, Kingcote's most searching early definition of himself:

> I pass my days in a dream, which too often becomes a nightmare. It is very likely you are right, and that with every day thus spent I only grow more incapable of activity, instead of making advance by a perception of what I could and ought to do. I find myself regarding with a sort of dull amazement every species of active and creative work. A childish wonder at the commonest things besets me. For example I fall a-thinking on

this cottage in which I live, speculating as to who may have originally built it; and then it strikes me as curious that I dwell beneath its roof, waking and sleeping, with such complete confidence, taking for granted that the workmanship was good, the material sound, no flaw here or there which will some day bring the timbers down upon my head. It leads me on to architecture in general; I ponder on huge edifices, and stand aghast before the skill and energy embodied in them. In them and in all the results of the world's work, the sum of human endeavour weighs upon me, something monstrous, inexplicable. I try to realise the motive force which can have brought about such results, and come only to the conclusion that I am not as other men, that I lack the primal energies of human life.

(I, ix)

The pessimism here, that ultimate detachment from the illusion of life which is Kingcote's intellectual commitment, is defined first as a psychological state and then gropingly assessed with analytic detachment ("I lack the primal energies"). Much of the novel has this air of a diary in which a certain commitment tries to come to terms with its consequences. As a result, *Isabel Clarendon* is both a valuable guide to Gissing's thinking in the 'eighties and at the same time an updated version of the romantic "confession". But it is also trying to be more than that. By introducing a motive into his life, the feudal dream of the Lady of Knightswell who can become the object both of his romantic nostalgia and of his romantic rebellion (for Isabel is the object both of an adoration which is political and a pity which is morally energising), Gissing is portraying the descent of a metaphysic into the realm of actuality mediated through a dream. The dream crumbles: Isabel is a much humbler character than Kingcote's conception of her demands, and this too has the makings of a successful novel. It is just that it is not Gissing's kind of novel. The fact that it is so tempting to see it as a kind of *Werther* (more so I think than the more obvious models offered by Turgenev) makes this clear. The novel, for all its Schopenhauerian gestures, offers a very simple dichotomy between illusion and reality. Can the woman I dreamt of exist? She does but she is not what I dreamt. The illusions of Gissing's novels are very different from this. The phrase about primal energies foreshadows

83

the ways in which they will differ. Life does not present this kind of choice: to opt out of a given mode of social action is merely to become trapped in another. Kingcote is one of the unclassed, but he is never made to occupy that determined space: it is occupied only vicariously by his sister on the one hand, and Isabel on the other.

A *Life's Morning* is primarily concerned with the same ideological dilemma of the unclassed as *Isabel Clarendon* and like that novel it focusses on a single protagonist, Emily Hood who is a governess caught between the free country house world of her employer and the "shadow of home" which is that of the industrial lower middle class. The plot of the novel owes a great deal to Charlotte Brontë—Emily is loved and proposed to by the nephew of her employer, Wilfrid Athel, an Oxford undergraduate with a brilliant career ahead of him. She is sent home and there wooed by her father's employer, Dagworthy, who tries to trap her by making it look as though her father has embezzled money. When she refuses to comply, charges are preferred and her father commits suicide, and she feels bound to renounce her wealthy lover both because of the disgrace and in order to nurse her neurotic mother. Six years later, Wilfrid, a successful politician engaged to the upper-class woman he had rejected for Emily, meets the heroine, poor, ill and above all regretting her renunciation. The novel drifts into a sugary ending.

The novel has this romantic melodrama for its structure, but at least the ideological exploration is distanced to the extent that it is focussed on the mind of a woman on the edge of her adulthood. Maybe this too is derivative from Charlotte Brontë, but what is very different is the texture of circumstance. The forms of oppression are specific. The world of Emily's employer is liberal and humane, but crucially exclusive, and the very presence of the governess draws the line of its limitation. At the same time it is contrasted in its freedom with the slavery of the industrial world. On the one hand, we have Wilfrid and Emily's rival feeling frustrated by the amount of choice offered them: "my despair," Wilfrid tells Emily, "is the universality of my interests" (I), and he tells Beatrice that she has to choose between being "a queen in drawing-rooms" and being "a real artist"—"by trying to be a bit of everything you become insignificant" (II). On the other hand, the world of Emily's home is a world where choice is constricted. One of the best aspects of the novel, and one that foreshadows most clearly the later Gissing, is the way in which Hood's fate is determined by a complex meshing of circumstance and trivial weakness which is almost comic: the money is planted on him, he breaks into it because his hat blows away and he feels bound to buy a new one, and he spends the rest of it because he meets an old friend who takes him for a drink from which he has abstained for many years and so grown unused to it. The irony is that the episode of the drinking is a single moment of self assertion in a life that is totally oppressed: "Having been so often treated like a dog, he had come to expect such treatment, and, what was worse, but feebly to resent it. He had lost the conscious dignity of manhood; nay, had perhaps never possessed it, for his battle had begun at so early an age" (IX). The logic that leads from being in a trap to closing the trap around oneself because you know that it will close anyway is typical of the way in which Gissing's ideological pessimism transforms itself into a fictional exposure of social oppression. For here it is tied to a specific mode of social relationships. Thus when Hood is pleading with Dagworthy, Gissing comments:

> Not for an instant did he falter in his purpose, but it gave him pleasure to be thus prayed to. The employer of labour is not as a rule troubled with a lively imagination; a pity, for it would surely gratify him to feel in its fulness at times his power of life and death. Native defect and force of habit render it a matter of course that a small population should eat or starve at his pleasure; possibly his resolution in seasons of strike is now and then attributable to awakening of insight and pleasure in prolonging his role of hunger god. (XIII)

Despite its bitterness, such a remark is, of course, very much in the tradition of Carlyle and Dickens which imagines that the evils of capitalism derive from the character of capitalists, and not vice versa, but at least it generalises Dagworthy who for most of the novel, as his name suggests, is a melodramatic villain. And since what is important is his power, it links with the descriptions of the oppressive environment and oppressed psychologies of the industrial world.

But although this is an isolated episode in the novel, it is also related to the novel's central concern; its ideological exploration of the concept of what constitutes "a life". What attracts Wilfrid to Emily is the perception of an individuality which betrays itself "even under the disadvantage of complete self-suppression" (I). Later he tells Beatrice that "there is a self in every one of us; the end of our life is to discern it, bring it out, make it actual" (II). Dagworthy's passion for Emily is defined as "reckless egoism", and she sees it not as love but as "a terrible possession" (VIII), but Gissing comments that this judgment derives from her inadequate knowledge of life. Indeed her own cult of the religion of beauty which is for her the inward expression of precisely that "self" is linked explicitly to "the note of our time", "intellectual egoism" (V). The presence of Meredith here is obvious but problematic. For Dagworthy's egoism is not the primitive egoism which founds property by brute force; he represents an intermediate stage between "the hard-headed operative who conquers wealth" and "his descendent who shall know what use to make of it" (VIII). It is this limited emancipation which attracts him to Emily: his passion is a sign both of his ruthlessness and his capability of refinement. In Meredith, egoism is possessive, but it has to be opposed not by altruism but by a non-possessive egoism which he can define in terms of sexual prowess and awakening. But for Gissing, such an awakening can only be another form of oppression (we could explain this ideologically by saying that an admirer of Schopenhauer could not share Meredith's faith in *natura naturans*, or offer Gissing credit for understanding the way in which sexual passion is made an agent of a mode of production through marriage, which is certainly clear in *The Odd Women*, and implied in Ida Starr, and the comments about Emily's mother). Emily's egoism therefore takes a different, topical form, which is a more or less explicit Paterian cult of beauty: "It is the art of life to take each moment of mental joy, of spiritual openness, as though it would never be repeated, to cling to it as a pearl of great price, to exhaust its possibilities of sensation" (III). What poses itself as a question, the ideological question of the novel, is that of the contingency of such a mode of thought: "Could her soul retain its ideal of beauty if environed by ugliness?" (V). It poses itself fictionally in the shadow of a home which is not only ugly but which is vulnerable to oppression.

When Wilfrid makes his statement about the self, he contrasts Napoleon the Great who may have been a curse to mankind, "but one thinks more of him than of Napoleon the Little, who wasn't quite sure whether to be a curse or a blessing" (II), but this is in the context of the liberal country home. The basic ideological statement about the self is precisely exposed when Emily is confronted with the reckless egoism of her local Napoleon. She has only reached her Paterian poise by striving; "her nature concealed a darker strain, an instinct of asceticism which now and again predominated, especially in the period of her transition to womanhood when the material conditions of her life were sad and of little hope" (III). The notion of material conditions calling forth a darker strain is crucial, and what is interesting here is that this is not left, as in the case of Maud Enderby, as a dualism, but is integrated with the ideal of beauty to become the kind of aestheticism that we find in the late work of Pater, in, for example, Marius the Epicurean which appeared in the very year in which Gissing was writing A Life's Morning. Specific material conditions compel her to make of her self-consciousness a work of art, which accounts for the moments of lassitude when the rugged baldness of life stripped of illusion asserts itself (XI) as well as the moments of spiritual joy. To make of life a work of art is to offer a specific resistance to material conditions, and this last quotation is from a chapter entitled "Emily's Decision". Confronted with "the very end of the rapturous dream which has lulled you whilst destiny wrought your woe", Emily faces the spectre of her aspiring self and thinks of Claudio and Isabella (Pater's essay on Measure for Measure is relevant here). The religion of beauty becomes a religion of chastity, the cult of spiritual joy is preserved by renunciation. The specific resistance to material conditions becomes an abrogation of the materialisation of the dream that destiny denies.

I am stressing the Paterian quality of Emily's existential adventure in order to show the way in which Gissing asserts the metaphysic, or ideology, of the unclassed as a function of material determinants, and how he achieves it in this novel by siting the aspiration in a gap between the "free" but exclusive upper world and the circumstantial world of industrial capitalism. For Emily is both a victim of circumstance and an example of specific resistance to it. But it goes further than this. For Emily, renunciation is a way of surviving with some self-respect, but at the end of six years, she comes to recognise that it is a self-respect bought at the cost of herself. In one way it is the most Meredithian moment of the novel:

> Aid against this sublety of conscience rose in the form of self-reproof administered by that joyous voice of nature which no longer timidly begged a hearing, but came as a mandate from an unveiled sovereign . . . That part in life alone becomes us which is the expression of ourselves. What merit can there be in playing the votary of an ascetic conviction when the heart is bursting with its stifled cry for light and warmth, for human joy, for the golden fruit of the tree of life? (XXIV).

The chapter is called "The Unexpected" and the question posed here is rhetorical because the novelist has intervened on Emily's behalf with a god from the fictional machine. She does not have to put this question to her original decision. But it is the question of Gissing's question. That is, that the unclassed, being zoned, answer to their awareness with the answer that they are given—keep apart, keep apart and preserve your soul alive. But that is the ideology of Gissing's protagonists. They answer against their oppression in a way that they are called on to answer, but the unasked question of that answer is the stifled cry for light and warmth. Gissing thought *Isabel Clarendon* and *A Life's Morning* had side-tracked him from his main concern as a novelist. And this is true, but it is a very necessary side-tracking. The artistic awareness which is the ideology of the unclassed remains something apart, something disconnected from the material conditions of their being, until, by shifting that awareness into the centre, he has entrammelled it in the social structure he portrays. In *A Life's Morning* we have a great step forward because that structure specifically sites the existential predicament in the class and sexual oppressions of industrial capitalism, and exposes through and beyond the ideology of that awareness the rigour of material determinants.

In this sense, *Demos* is not a return to the mainstream, but a logical consequence of *A Life's Morning*. Indeed, its major focus, that of the industrialisation of English life, grows directly out of the sections on Emily's home, and the whole country house ideology that is set up as a normative alternative to socialism (which is effectively indistinguishable from capitalism) is prepared for by *Isabel Clarendon*. Essentially, Gissing is writing for the same virtual public in all three novels, a public represented by the Harrisons and the Gaussens who could afford to be as critical of industrial oppression as they were frightened of working-class independence. If anything, *Demos*, is less honest than the other two, because the ideologically exponent character, Hubert Eldon, is able to direct all his intellectual "rebellion" against the working class, and finds no contradiction in restoring the cosy feudal façade of the rentier class to its pristine pastoral beauty. At least in the two preceding novels the fiction is open enough to allow us to see the limitations of that class, at least Kingcote and Emily stand opposed to its exclusivity and conventionalism. Neither is it typical of Gissing to portray industrial capitalism in its manufacturing phase. The descriptions of Dunfield and Wanley are too mediated by Carlyle to have, say, the vitality of Mrs. Gaskell. What is important about *Demos* in the development of Gissing is something that is continued and extended from *A Life's Morning*, the foreshortened awakening of the oppressed woman, Adela, into the trammels of social actuality. It is extended importantly because Adela's sense of oppression is linked with the oppression of the working-class girl Emma Vine, and the spokesman for both is, as it were, the mother of the oppressor, Mrs. Mutimer. A group of women, coming from different classes but equally displaced from those classes—Stella Westlake, Adela, Emma, Mrs. Mutimer—hover questioningly on the edge of the novel's polemical narrative.

But through this connection, the novel achieves something else which is to be the centre of Gissing's effectivity. Emma and Mrs. Mutimer live out the contradictions voiced by Adela and Stella in a specific area of London. I have shown how this is beginning to happen in *The Unclassed*. Working-class London, however, is treated differently in that novel. Litany Lane is a slum enclave, a contaminated spot very similar to Dickens's Tom-All-Alone's—it has neither specific location nor inner differentials. It is not a containing zone, a function of the network of boundaries that constitute the modern city. Hoxton, however, has these features. It is realised as an area just as St. Marylebone is in *The Unclassed*, and because it is also realised as an area with a demographic identity more sharply focussed than the mixture of *The Unclassed*, it becomes also, if only fragmentarily, the site of the exploration of a group with a specific problematic. Hoxton is the best thing about *Demos*, and it is in the end on the margins of the novel. But it is very important, and very different from what has gone before. It launches Gissing into the next stage of his evolution, the achievement of his London through the realisation of the London of the urban poor. Not the slum so much as the ghetto, and from the ghetto he will emerge as the first novelist of the modern city, the forerunner, if never consciously acknowledged, of Dreiser and Joyce, and the line of writers who have made fictions of the urban revolution. We must now attend to this development in the two finest of Gissing's early novels, *Thyrza* and *The Nether World*.

4

"He taught people a certain way of regarding the huge city"— Gissing's tribute to Dickens's value as the novelist of London has the more weight precisely because he has spent much of his own career portraying aspects of London life, and because he has portrayed them so differently from Dickens. For if Dickens is vivid it is partly because he is picturesque, and Gissing is clearly not. However, it would be naïve to assume that because he himself portrays London with no sense of its imaginative propensities, that he therefore portrays it more accurately. On the contrary, there is a sense in which the photographic reproduction of the ordinary is achieved in language only by a certain verbal distance, most flagrantly evident in, say, the classical allusions ironically used in the description of bank holiday in *The Nether World*, but present also in more routine linguistic strategies. For example, at the very opposite of the ironic rhetoric is the very bald and detailed naming of streets and buildings. You can trace the movements of Gissing's characters on a map of London and this seems to constitute a kind of objectivity, an unmediated mimesis by which the story is placed in an actual terrain, as though he doesn't want to fictionalise the context. But the effect of this, as with much naturalistic description, is to make that

90

terrain "exotic" rather than representative. You won't recognise anything about it unless you know it, and the rhetorical relationship between the author and the reader assumes that you won't know it. One way of describing the difference between Dickens's London and Gissing's is to say that Dickens establishes a world the reader can enter, so much so that Gissing himself first saw London through Dickens's eyes, while Gissing makes a report back.

Certain features of Dickens's London make it into an imaginative world. First, the organisation of space in Dickens is based on a tension between obscurity and proximity. The city is specifically an agglomeration, so much so that its crowdedness creates areas of darkness which are stressed by the hierarchical distances of the social structure. Thus its capacity for suspense, drama, the sheltering of evil, derives from unknown contingencies which only the author with his synoptic vision, as the scribe of a whole social world, can uncover and manipulate. Secondly, the city is a palimpsest, an overlapping multiplicity of functions—rule, commerce, manufacture, or simply the redistribution of surplus (which is served primarily by crime at one end of society, and expropriation at the other)—and overwritten histories which inscribe themselves on archaic institutions and pursued lives. So that if space is full of unknown contingencies, time is loaded with obstruction and catastrophe only grasped by the author's right to make plots and establish denouements. Finally, the city is located in pastoral values. Urban as he is, Dickens, as Gissing realised, is always looking at the city in terms of his contrast with the country, with a rural past which always beckons back. These are crude generalisations, but they form the basis of "imagination" in any meaningful sense: for "imagination" entails the esemplastic power—the constituting of the disparate fragments of the seen as an organic whole—and this is only possible in a space whose lacunae can be leapt by vision, in a time whose disjunctions are underwritten with continuities, and above all in a world whose complexity can be held in a frame of value.

Gissing has none of this. His London, though it might be unfamiliar, is not unknown—it is charted, literally mapped out, and that mapping creates distances which have no contingency. The distances have to be travelled, the districts lie next to one another, not stacked like squares of wheat as in Philip Larkin's deliberately

91

idealised image,[2] but as zones functioning as class and economic differentials. And although historic London is evoked, it is usually only to remind us that the history is forgotten. There is no Court of Chancery, no Circumlocution Office, no centre whose obstructiveness folds in the passage of time like the coil of a spring. Characters are caught in daily lives, as they are enclosed in zoned spaces. The novels, especially in the 'eighties, are full of plots that come to nothing, as though the organic time of the novelist is defeated by the mechanical time of economic exigency, just as the effective space of the palimpsest is replaced by the created space of productive and consumptive functions. Clerkenwell and Lambeth, or for that matter Camberwell, are not thrown up by the tangle of history, they are made because industry needs workers, and capitalism needs markets. This is why there is so little sense of class relations in Gissing—for such relations cannot be located in human contacts, however rigidly controlled. They are embodied rather in the mediated demands and accommodation of streets, factories and trades. Chancery may be inhuman, but to be inhuman requires its negation, the human. Gissing's city is rather non-human, an indifferent terrain which acts like a fate. For all its overcrowding, it is as it is imaged, a curiously empty city. You take the crowds for granted—what you are conscious of is the manipulation of physical geography. It is not in any sense an imaginative city.

The most succinct summary of the differences between Gissing and Dickens from this point of view is Adrian Poole's: "The city has been drained of its epistemological excitement; the blank streets, the gritty light, the coarse sounds, seem to provoke sullen resignation rather than vigilant expectancy" (pp. 41–2). He links this with an ideological transformation, the increasing isolation of the observing self which with Gissing, as with many of his contemporaries, emerges as a failure of language of the kind just noted (ironic aloofness, or exotic reportage) that consolidates rather than overcomes distances. Gissing's value, for Poole, is that, unlike some of his contemporaries, he stares across the lines of separation with enough clarity and intensity for us to be conscious of the desire to uncover the "human reality" beneath class differences, but still we lack an "extension of perception and feeling." Gissing tends, in this argument (which is certainly important and convincing), to become a second best Dickens—faced with an intensifying alienation, he is unable to combat it, but at least he realises its dangers. I have been arguing, however, that it is precisely what makes Gissing unlike Dickens that constitutes his effectiveness, and I want to try to establish that although we are faced with a very different London in Gissing, that this is because his London is not mid-Victorian London, and because he has a very different fictional task from Dickens, a task which cannot be identified as the assimilation of knowledge into a "human reality".

The difference between Dickens and Gissing can be related to the differences between the two great sociologists of London with whose work their novels are roughly contemporary. In fact, Eileen Yeo's criticism of Booth (*The Unknown Mayhew*, pp. 102–9) resembles, in a number of ways, Poole's criticism of Dickens. Essentially both argue that the two later writers are characterised by an apparent objectivity which merely covers an ideologically controlled distance from their observed material. We must try to understand the way in which this distance works in Booth in order to have a precise sense of the ideological formation of Gissing and what possibilities it releases, for although Gissing's most important writings on working-class London precede the first appearance of Booth, he shares the same intellectual climate and confronts the same city. More than this, Booth[3] makes very clear the ideological shaping of his knowledge in his concern for methodology. Thus, for example, he is explicit about the way in which his conception of knowledge actually excludes certain kinds of evidence:

At the outset we shut our eyes, fearing lest any prejudice of our own should colour the information we received. It was not till the books were finished that I or my secretaries ourselves visited the streets amongst which we had been living in imagination. But later we gained confidence, and made it a rule to see each street ourselves at the time we received the visitors' account of it. With the insides of houses and their inmates there was no attempt to meddle. To have done so would have been an unwarrantable impertinence; and, besides, a contravention of our understanding with the School Board, who object, very rightly, to any abuse of the delicate machinery with which they work. Nor for the same reason, did we ask the visitors to obtain information specially for us. We dealt solely with that which comes to them in a natural way in the discharge of their duties.

(I, 25)

The vocabulary reveals an extreme scientificity—shutting one's eyes for fear that they will colour the truth, remaining outside the lives of the people, as though the observer is necessarily kept at a photographic distance, not seeking information but only taking what comes in a "natural" way. It denotes an epistemology of extreme empiricism, and at the same time a kind of idealism which only trusts knowledge which is mediated; and epistemology of the resolutely detached observer. Booth openly acknowledges the limits of this knowledge. At the end of the first volume, he says that the survey is confined to "how things are" and does not concern itself with how they got there or where they are going. But if there is no history, neither is there any depth: "to interpret the life of either (individual or class), we need to lay open its memories and understand its hopes" (I, 593), but the facts presented do not attempt that. Indeed, the empirical evidence itself is doctored to produce an impression of averageness:

> The materials for sensational stories lie plentifully in every book of our notes; but, even if I had the skill to use my material in this way—that gift of imagination which is called "realistic"— I should not wish to use it here . . . My object has been to attempt to show the numerical relation which poverty, misery, and depravity bear to regular earnings and comparative comfort, and to describe the general conditions under which each class lives.
>
> (I, 6)

That linking of realism and sensationalism, the commitment to the numerical relation and general conditions show how determined Booth is that the survey should not be ruffled by an actual sense of what it means to be poor.

Not surprisingly, this epistemology is related to a tacit social doctrine, despite denials that the evidence is approached without theory. The rather crude, pre-experimental scientism is backed up, as Yeo says, by a biologistic and moralistic ethic which amounts effectively to a political commitment. At the basis of the survey is an entirely static concept of class. Booth's classes are in fact categories which lie on top of one another and which consist of spaces through which the individual passes by virtue of his fitness to survive. There is no real sense of classes having a functional relationship to a mode of production. The dividing line in society thus becomes the boundary between two zones—poverty on one side and sufficiency on the other. What emerges from this is that although the percentage of people living in poverty is much higher than expected (30%), it constitutes no major threat to the social structure, not certainly the kind of threat that many read into the riots of 1886 and 1887. Nevertheless, there is a muddled fear that naïve charity, socialist agitation, and a social competitiveness that is too absolute, might combine to excerbate the problems latent in the social process. Social action must be confined to encouraging temperance and thrift so that the observed difference between those "who actually suffer from poverty" and "the true working classes, whose desire for a larger share of wealth is of a different character" can be cultivated. The danger of agitation is that it elides this difference: "it is not by welding distress and aspirations that any good can be done" (I, 155). Booth's specific proposals reflect this faint fear of socialism. He divides the working class into six "classes" of which two, A and B, are below the poverty line; two, C and D, are on it; and two E and F, above it. Most of the problems of poverty come from the pressure on C and D (who have intermittent earnings and small regular earnings respectively) exerted by the presence of A and B, so that if we can eliminate A (a small class of occasional labourers, loafers and criminals) and take B out of the social process by a limited form of social welfare, C and D will find the struggle to survive less vexed by chance and despair:

> The poverty of the poor is mainly the result of the competition of the very poor. The entire removal of this very poor class out of the daily struggle for existence I believe to be the only solution of the problem.
>
> (I, 154)

The daily struggle for existence, however, remains the norm. Booth's scientism is a commitment to a modified capitalism.

We have to acknowledge this kind of distancing not merely as an epistemological limitation but as a function of the demands of the higher organisation of capitalism to naturalise its social relations of production as "the daily struggle for existence", but I think that ideology is not merely a limitation, it is also a way of seeing. And Booth, if he lacks Mayhew's sharp insight into the lives of the poor, if more than this he is naïve about class relations, has another value quite different from Mayhew. That loss of human contact, that reduction of Class to categories of space, enables a distinctive contribution to the theory of urbanisation which is vital for our understanding of Gissing. For Mayhew, as for Dickens, London is an experience, and because most of our responses to literary texts are in terms of experience, Booth seems a curiously unimaginative writer. But the city can only be experienced as a city as long as it can be seen, and there comes a time in the development of cities when this is very difficult because of its expansion and its change of function. In the mid-Victorian period, London is still primarily an administrative and redistributive city. By the time of Gissing and Booth it is a generative city with its own productive function and its own markets. When Mayhew looks down on London from St. Paul's, he is seeing it as a place—it can be grasped as an experience because it has an outside. The generative city is like a universe, however, a self-contained system of distances and zones which interrelate not with another world, but with one another. To put it another way, we are speaking not of an identifiable object, the city, but of a total process,[4] urbanisation, which begins to invade the countryside. It seems to me no accident that Booth's survey first appears in the same year as *Tess of the D'Urbervilles*, a novel which records the urbanisation of country life. Thus, the city itself has to be analysed as a spatial organisation. And in a sense, it is unfair to look to Booth for its anthropology when its distinctive value is topographical. It is very significant that the final metaphor of the introduction is that of photography, which is not naïvely conceived of as a mimetic technique:

> As in photographing a crowd, the details of the picture change continually, but the general effect is much the same, whatever moment is chosen. I have attempted to produce an instantaneous picture, fixing the facts on my negative as they appear at a given moment, and the imagination of my readers must add the movement, the constant changes, the whirl and turmoil of life.
>
> (I. 27)

The photograph is a piece of specifically limited evidence, the making of a stasis from the mobility of experience, a process of abstraction. And the abstraction in Booth is not the individual life, but the social space of a demographic process, the structure of an urban universe. Harold Pfautz's[5] essay on Booth shows precisely this. Booth, he says, makes two major innovations. First, by making an enquiry into distribution patterns made by class, occupation, and "the general law of successive migration", he is able to identify the forces which determine these patterns: population increase, excess of immigration, business expansion, developing standards of living, and such special factors as transport facilities, lie of the land, constitution of the family and localisation of labour. Secondly, he establishes areal units, of which the most important are "analytic areal constructs" made possible through the understanding of boundaries, barriers, social character (population's type, physical site, type of institution) and situation (accessibility, etc.). In this way, Booth establishes the city as a spatial order: urbanisation as a process is analysed in terms of the structure it determines, the map it draws. Booth could not, obviously, have seen this had he not committed himself to a specific mode of distance which is that of the natural scientist—in short, to the structuration of agglomerated human interactions. This in turn depends on seeing class relations as a dehumanised state. In the truly urbanised city, lives are fought out in zones, individual dramas in the context of a given structure which constitutes effectively an intractable universe.

Thus, in Booth, a conscious self-distancing means two things: first, an ideological distortion, a false consciousness which reifies the social order; but second, a way of seeing which, in comparison with Mayhew, takes account of the city as a spatial order reflecting a total process (urbanisation). If we are to understand Gissing's fiction we need to relate this to his way of presenting London. Gissing shares many of Booth's insights, and much of his ideology. Above all, he shares that distance which leaves city life to appear as a biological phenomenon, a structured space in which individuals survive or die caught in behaviour patterns that can no more be changed by minor contingencies than a polar bear's fur can be turned brown by being born in the London Zoo—biology is not Lamarckian in the late nineteenth century.

But, because he is a novelist, and therefore entangled with the subjective experience of this biology, what tends to appear a complacency in Booth is sharply ironised recognition in Gissing. Booth states, for example, that the lives of classes C and D are "an unending struggle . . . but I do not know that they lack happiness" (I, 131). Most of the protagonists of Gissing's working-class novels fall within that category, and it is clear that such happiness is either a fleeting illusion or the product of an effective ruthlessness or insensitivity. Equally, some of the recommendations of the survey, such as Octavia Hill's injunction that a housing policy should "scatter rather than intensify" (II, 264), is realised with all its implications for the quality of living in *The Nether World* when Sidney and Clara Kirkwood are taken from the acute depression of Clerkenwell to the slow attrition of isolation in Crouch End. Many individual points like this can be made about Gissing's work in relation to Booth. Gissing's concern with the nature of slums, the ironies of luxury production, the unemployed, the ambiguities of model dwellings, the distorting eye of philanthropy, are all confirmed by Booth, as is the detailed description of specific districts and even streets. Booth paid tribute to *Demos* (I, 57), and *Thyrza* and *The Nether World* especially are vindicated again and again by Booth's survey as an accurate picture of London life. At the same time, he shares the same distance without any of the ideological comforts of the sociologist.

But what is more important is that Gissing makes fictions out of the spatial order of the city as a totality. There can be no synoptic image, because what concerns him is precisely the patterns of areal distribution which hold industrial and commercial London together. His novels are based on maps, fictional terrains which are equivalents of analytic areal constructs. It is not London that constitutes the setting of his novels but Hoxton or Lambeth or Clerkenwell whose definition is made by reference outward to other areas of London, Islington or Bloomsbury or Westminster, so that what characterises the setting is what separates them within the urban universe. Even when, as in *Thyrza*, somewhere outside London like Eastbourne becomes a point of reference, it tends to be presented as another, wealthier suburb, and when, in some of the later novels, characters go away from London to a country area it is usually *on holiday*, which is merely the middle-class equivalent of the excursion, the contained time which reflects the enclosed nature of the park. So there is no city and country theme (especially after the very immature *Isabel Clarendon* and *Demos*) but only a system of mobility and fixity. And once the "regional" working-class novels give way to the middle-class novels, and the degree of mobility is increased, we still have no sense of a unified place but only distances to be traversed, locations which define an economic situation: Regent's Park to Islington, Walworth to Herne Hill, and so on. The relationship of fixity and mobility is based on the system of distances and conjunctions which organise the space of the terrain, and in the early novels particularly we have a strong sense of intramural boundaries—Regents Canal (*Demos*), the river as an object to cross (rather than to go along) in *Thyrza*, the non-residential vacuum of Bloomsbury which buffers Clerkenwell from the West End in *The Nether World*. You cross these boundaries into new areas which mark themselves out by non-pervasion. Thus a very modest migration, from Clerkenwell to Islington, for example, entails a whole set of social mutations. This areal significance reflects the social relations of the inhabitants. Great stress is laid in Booth's survey by his researchers on the differentials in industry (Clara Collett's description of a factory girl is an important case in point) and on the hidden ironies of the contrast between the worker and his beneficiaries who people the consumer zone of the same city (Beatrice Potter makes the same point about dockers that Gissing makes about the jewellery trade—that the contiguity and connection of supplier and user only emphasises the distance in life-style and environment). This is not Dickens's kind of proximity—there is no sense that the underworld might suddenly erupt into the complacency of the dominant classes, merely that it is close and apart, at a distance inexorably governed by a mode of production. That is the precise significance of the structure of the generative city, the city of Booth and Gissing. Space is structured to guarantee the divisions on which it rests.

But this is to talk about the London Gissing is to arrive at, and it is not there ready-made. On the contrary, it only emerges as a fictional solution to the problems that pose themselves throughout the novels of the 'eighties. From very early on, Gissing is, as we have seen, very conscious of the determinant role of class, and to begin with, he attempts to realise this in the manner of the mid-Victorian novel in terms of a dramatic confrontation—Arthur and Helen, Waymark and Ida, Mutimer and Adela, and so on. Equally, however, London proves intractable because the relationships which it makes possible are not cognate with class relationships. The characters of *The Unclassed* are both bound by their roles in society—teacher, prostitute, rent-collector, and so on—but also form an unclassed community through the casual contiguity of the London streets. Thus they tend to wander about London without much rhyme or reason. After the startling opening with its sense of streets which represent the social structure, and journeys which confirm the distance between the social categories, the physical structure of London has little to do with the lives of the protagonists. *Demos* focusses more narrowly on an area, and on class relationships, but Gissing cannot hold the two together. The reason is not difficult to see. I pointed out earlier that class relationships as functions of a mode of production were just what Booth doesn't photograph. The social space of the city, insofar as it is created space (which is more and more true as the city stops serving the country and becomes an end in itself, enclosing its own production and consumption), is partly organised to keep class relationships to an abstraction—suburbs, ghettoes, thoroughfares are all ways of keeping the possibilities of direct confrontation at bay. So that if Booth is going to reflect the social space of the city, it must be by the repression of relationships, the whirl of life, and class must be but the personification of zoning. Gissing's solution is ultimately not to combat the physical structure of the city in order to personalise class relations, but to use that structure precisely to fictionalise the reification of those relations.

The working out of this is most evident in *Thyrza*. Gissing's fifth novel, it is set in Lambeth, or more precisely the area bordered by the river, Westminster Bridge Road, Kennington Road and Broad Street, and is the story of Walter Egremont, guilt-ridden heir of his father's oilcloth works who tries to start evening classes for his workmen, but instead falls in love with the betrothed of his best pupil and librarian, Gilbert Grail. He decides to break off the romance which more or less destroys both heroine and lover. Thyrza is rescued by a benevolent friend of Egremont and returns to Grail, but only to die. The plot thus has all the makings of a drama of class relationships, but it is also a very thin and sentimental story which in fact is little more than a pretext for the portrayal of life in Lambeth. "I am living at present in Lambeth," Gissing wrote in 1886, "doing my best to get at the meaning of that strange world so remote from our civilisation" (*Letters*, p. 187). Egremont in fact has to play a double role—agent of the middle-class, he is also the displaced consciousness abroad in a remote zone (though it is only just across the river). The class relationships have to be personalised within this assumption of distance.

It is a great advance on *Demos*, because it makes the confrontation take place between the industrial capitalist and the worker, rather than between the aristocrat and the worker-become-capitalist, and it takes place in the area of its origin rather than in a distant rural world. Moreover, if Egremont is an unusual capitalist, he has a context in the whole intellectual imperialism of the philanthropic and education movements which dominated the eighteen-eighties—Toynbee Hall, the People's Palace, and so on. For such movements take working-class London as a *problem* (the eighteen-eighties is the decade of dramatic metaphors—"darkest London", "the maiden tribute to modern Babylon"), and this in itself is an index of social distance. "What if his life were to be a struggle between inherited sympathies and the affinities of his intellect? All the better, perchance, for his prospect of usefulness; he stood as a mediator between two sections of society. But for his private happiness, how?" (VII). Egremont is truly the son of an industrial capitalist, involved in and yet intellectually and financially removed from the processes of production. Part of the novel's strength is that it establishes this paradox with unusual irony. Egremont is trying to bring Culture to the working class, but they already have a culture as the "friendly lead" shows. It is true, as Poole (p. 78) shows, that Gissing's observation of working-class life, which is rich and informed in this novel, is enclosed in an idiom of "a generalised and distancing compassion" ("if they lacked refinement it was not their fault . . ." the narrator comments). But the whole established reality of working-class life also measures the ambiguity of Egremont's concern—his philanthropy, as Mrs. Ormonde tells him, is not heroic. It is significant that what draws Egremont to Thyrza is her voice, and that, in the end, his passion for her is limited, an aesthetic ideal ultimately which doesn't become any more heroic than his social conscience: "You were tried, Mr. Egremont, and found wanting" (XLI).

Thus the double role of Egremont, agent of knowledge, agent of reform, is up to a certain point fictionally very fruitful, because it precisely reflects the problematic of the class relationship in a zoned city. The contradictory desire in Egremont, to emancipate the working-class world, and to possess it through love, builds up an intolerable tension in the first twenty-four chapters of the novel. Furthermore, unlike *Demos*, the working-class world is not limited to an ideological function. Grail and Thyrza are not merely sports, because they live their lives among characters who have their own distinctive vitality: Lydia, Totty Nancarrow, Luke Ackroyd, Mrs. Poole, even Bunce, are not externally portrayed—they have a psychology as well as a biology and this makes the personalisation of class relationships possible. The contact is broken, in fact, by the middle-class world. The inhumanity of Dalmaine, the scheming of Mrs. Ormonde and, above all, the passivity of Egremont himself conspire to make Lambeth a separate and obscure world. If the novel becomes broken-backed once the crisis in Egremont's relationship with Thyrza has been reached, it is because at that point the novel can only logically go one of two ways—towards romance or towards cruelty. Through intrigue, Dalmaine's exposure of the truth and Mrs. Ormonde's complex stratagem to get Thyrza out of the way, the denouement is taken out of Lambeth, to the Caledonian Road, to Eastbourne. Lambeth is sealed off. Any vitality the novel has after this point is in the tissue of minor stories which take place in this sealed off Lambeth—Lyddy and Ackroyd, Totty and Bunce, and so on. Meanwhile Thyrza's death, which is effectively an apotheosis, is the price paid on behalf of Egremont's vacillity. The plot foreshadows Tess and Angel, and indeed much of the novel is implicitly asking questions about the nature of woman. But, of course, in Hardy's novel, that sexual conflict is deeply embedded in the economic structure. In *Thyrza*, it is taken out of the domain of class confrontation at precisely the point where it threatens to open up the class conflict.

102

And yet if this is the novel's failure, it is a failure which is instructive. For the sealing off of Lambeth is not merely a backing away, it is also the basis of a recognition. The sign of this recognition is a physical location—Lambeth Bridge. Grail is our first register after he has heard from Egremont that he is made librarian in Egremont's scheme and thus taken out of the rut of factory work. The passage in Chapter IX begins with Grail in Lambeth Walk stopping to listen to a street organ, "that music of the obscure ways" which speaks for "all that is purely human in these darkened multitudes" (which is not some kind of transcendent passion, but is the expression of desire, revolt and striving for enjoyment before the darkness of the future). It is the "secret of hidden London", you can only know it if you make yourself at one with "those who dwell around . . . in the unmapped haunts of the semi-human". Later, of course, Egremont hears Thyrza singing, and this too is the music of obscurity. But it is Grail, no outsider, who listens to the organ, a privileged moment for the reader who will watch Egremont destroying what he wants to emancipate and love. After this, Grail reaches the bridge to the music of the parish church bells, "a harsh peal of four notes, endlessly repeated". The bridge itself is ugly, its iron superstructure, mean by day, invested at night with a grim severity. If the organ suggests a human continuity, the bells and the bridge, the created symbols of the city, are hostile—harsh and severe. Grail walks out to the middle of the bridge and looks down river, along the other shore to Parliament ("obscure magnitude") and the "dim grey shape" of the Abbey, resting place of poets, which fills his heart with worship. Then the eye travels back along the south shore to the hospital (block after block) and the Archbishop's Palace, dark, lifeless. The shores are thus the sites of institutions, but what strikes us is their obscurity. In Westminster Dalmaine lives; a little further away, Egremont has his pied-à-terre. But Grail is not to cross—only to walk to the middle and contemplate the distant worlds of politics and culture. Finally there is only the eddying water and the piercing wind. He has gone out to "realise" the great joy which has befallen him, but he is drawn by an unknown power to this severe reminder that the other side is obscure, unreachable, and that there are other times when he could have wished that the water could take his life. An inexorability of structures frames a change-able tide. Later in the novel, it is the bridge that is the scene of Egremont's farewell to Thyrza. This time they almost cross to the other side, because Thyrza is confused by the jangle of bells. What they see on the other side is not Westminster but Millbank Peni-tentiary. When Egremont has indirectly broken off with Thyrza, he wishes that they had stayed on the Lambeth side where the bells allow "no delicacies of tone" (XXIV). After this, she hides in the parapet, so that he can't pursue her to the Lambeth side. And when he arrives there he meets Grail. Soon he stops worry-ing about Thyrza in his hurry to get away from Lambeth where his conscience is so exposed. But alone, he crosses the river via Westminster Bridge.

These are perhaps self-consciously symbolic passages. Gissing might seem to be using an equivalent of the great unifying images of Dickens's London. What is crucial, however, is that the bridge is a sign of distance, a distance which is natural, but which forms the basis of the social space of the city. The imagery which sur-rounds the bridge is counter to any sense that it might function as a means of communication: not the overcoming of space but the structuring of space. The road on it is narrow, as though to indicate that crossing is minimal. And this structuring is im-placable. The sealing off of Lambeth, which is the failure of the plot of the novel, is also a response to something more important —the constituent factor of Gissing's London, the physical shap-ing of social relationships by the created space of the industrial and generative city. It would be a more human place if the secret of hidden London was truly discoverable in a musical sound. But it is rather the mapping of the unmapped streets that opens it up, and maps designate a world structured by its physical in-stitutions, streets, buildings, bridges. Gissing's final solution to the problem of portraying class relations is in the novel which follows *Thyrza*, where the zoning off is accepted as a site of the fiction. The other world enters here only as an abstraction, money, motivating the greed and the suffering of an enclosed hell. I have discussed this novel at length in other essays,[6] and there is no point in repeating what I have already said. Its importance here is that it represents the final evolution of Gissing's London, a world of sealed off zones which replace the dramatic confrontations of Dickens's London with named streets, contrived distances. It is true that this reflects the ideology of Booth, of the late capitalist sociology. But there is this major difference, that Booth is almost exclusively concerned with a world that is other —darkest London. For Gissing, *The Nether World* is only a phase. It establishes the bases of a geography whose major feature is the distribution of the necessary but incommodious working-class. But it is a geography which has meaning too for the whole social structure, and the inexorability of the working-class zone is only a narrowly focussed prototype for the more complex inexorability of the unclassed. They share a common geography, though they have apparent freedom of movement. And in this respect, the ideological distance is to be differentiated from the distance necessary for the novelist. What is finally significant about Gissing is not that he can't reach beyond a certain point in his presentation of working-class life, but that he comes to the world of his own class knowing how the physical space of an urbanised world is what holds his characters finally in their places. The named streets of London map the fate of his protagonists.

5

A motif and a domain, then, separate Gissing from the realistic novels of the mid-century. The motif can be defined as the condition of being unclassed, as distinguished from being declassed, and this has several consequences. First, it means that Gissing's characters do not possess the middle of the social road—they are mobile but not travelling, and they occupy a marginal enclave which is both a determinant condition (in fact, superfluity) and a determinant psychology (polemical egotism). Second, the unclassed paradoxically constitute a kind of class—because it is not a privileged condition (as declassment is), the protagonist can only become an exposing agent, a register of a social world because he is part of a group. Class in Gissing cannot be defined in terms of consciousness, because class relations cannot be dramatised: class is therefore present as an unconsciously shared response to material conditions. The group in Gissing is evident in a shared function, or disfunction, which to the individual is only an abstract struggle against circumstances. The best example of this is *The Nether World* in which the working class operates in a sequence of internal rivalries and oppressions motivated by a single external form of oppression—poverty—which is common to everybody and derives from the relationship of the nether world to the upper. But it is equally true of the middle-class novels: Harriet and Ida, Isabel and Kingcote, Emily and Dagworthy, act out conflicts which are internalised versions of a common condition. The third consequence of the motif of the unclassed is one that is only resolved very slowly in the 'eighties, and that is that the specific identity given to the industrial working class by their role in production has to be matched in the group of the unclassed by a specific role which is generated as the "theme" of the novel. The early novels, *The Unclassed, A Life's Morning* and *Isabel Clarendon*, all have unclassment as a theme in itself, which is why they tend to have become more and more abstract rehearsals of ideas. But in the fully evolved Gissing novel it is transformed into a structuring principle which attaches itself to either a topic or the concept of a career (or both together). This is partly present already insofar as these three novels begin to use the theme to dramatise the problems of women in society —the prostitute, the governess, the protected wife—but the break really comes with *The Emancipated* in which Gissing is experimenting with the idea of a group placed by their social position in the confrontation between Hebraic and Hellenic cultural values.

But in another sense, *The Emancipated* is a parenthetical novel, written, one feels, as a relief from the intensity of *The Nether World*. A group of tourists vaguely trying to adapt to the challenge of classical, pagan art is not Gissing's *métier*. Significantly the only time at which the novel begins to have any life is when the heroine returns from abroad and lives in London. For Gissing's kind of London is an essential constituent of his fiction, because without that sense of zoning, of restricted mobility, of being placed by the names of streets, the unclassed are necessarily in a vacuum. What makes them reflective agents is marginality, but this marginality can only have meaning if it is enclosed within the urban world which produces it and accommodates it. Most of Gissing's major novels are special studies—the writer, the unmarried woman, the suburban family. But this specialisation is the key to Gissing's London. The zoned city fosters the zoned life, and although the very specific zoning of *The Nether World* is never repeated, his marginal people always have their lives mapped out by their very uncertainty of place. Is the nether world Clerkenwell or Hell?—is poverty a historical phenomenon or a metaphysical condition? The novel hinges on precisely that question. It does so because the city is no longer the meeting-place of the classes; on the contrary, it is the structured space of a separation and an abstraction. Because of this, it is those who are entangled in the interstices of that structure who light it up most graphically. Gissing wrote what is probably the best novel about working-class London in the late nineteenth century when he wrote *The Nether World*. But that is not what constitutes his importance as a novelist. It is rather that he is able to go on to make fictions which expose the determinants of the oppression so hopelessly given voice in that novel, not by personalising the class structure or by humanising its urban symbolism, but by inserting into it his own class of the unclassed and making them struggle to survive in the streets. Only London could create the unclassed, but only the unclassed can see London. A motif which is a point of view, the point of view of a specific ideology, but which is also a structure (the group, as opposed to the protagonist or the panorama), and which is also a plot (the story of a career, the story of a topical phenomenon), and a domain which is at once the location of these constituents and the object of their exposure—these are the elements of a Gissing novel.

By defining these elements, I hope I will have countered one very commonplace attitude to Gissing, and that is that he is a novelist whose interest is entirely thematic: formally, he writes slavishly within the conventions of the mid-Victorian novel. It is true that, in very superficial terms, Gissing's novels have plots and characters and that they present themselves to us as representations rather than artefacts. But no writer can be really interesting if what he has to realise is realisable within the forms available to him from writers of a previous generation. Gissing's novels are no more conventional than James's or Hardy's in this sense. On the contrary, it is precisely because of that "thematic" interest to which he has access, that Gissing is compelled to evolve a method of writing which violates the given forms in specific ways (most notably, the decentering of the protagonist, the demystification of landscape, and the thwarting of plots) and takes on its own identity. The presence in that identity of the most obvious features of "low mimetic" fiction is not because of Gissing's formal anonymity—it is precisely because those features constitute a fictive world that has to be overturned.

Because I want to stress this, the following chapters are devoted to close analyses of the novels which, together with *Born in Exile* and *The Nether World*, constitute the body of work by which Gissing has a claim on our attention. This means not dealing with some texts which are minor successes, such as *Denzil Quarrier* and *The Paying Guest*, or trying to account for the nature of the short stories (some of which are very fine). What seems to me to require emphasis is how close an analysis the major works repay.

NOTES

1 Benjamin, *Charles Baudelaire, A Lyric Poet in the Era of High Capitalism* (1973), pp. 35–6.
2 Larkin, *The Whitsun Weddings* (1964), p. 23.
3 Booth, *Labour and Life of the People*, 3rd edn. (1891). All references are to this edition.
4 See Lefebvre, *La Revolution Urbaine* (Paris, 1970). He elaborates the theory of urbanisation as a total process. There is a useful summary and critique of his argument in Harvey, op. cit., pp. 305–9.
5 See Booth, *On the City*, edited with an introduction by Harold Pfautz (Chicago, 1967).
6 Howard, Lucas, Goode, *Tradition and Tolerance in Nineteenth Century Fiction* (1966), pp. 207–41; Gissing, *The Nether World* (Brighton, 1974). Introduction, pp. V–XIV.

4

New Grub Street

1

In the third chapter of *New Grub Street*, Jasper Milvain, "man
of his day," and rising man of letters, walks in the countryside
with Marian Yule, the oppressed daughter of an embittered and
fanatical hack scholar to whose work she has to devote her life.
Both are on holiday from their literary labour in London, and
Milvain talks about the literary life, introducing the case of the
as yet absent hero of the novel, Edwin Reardon, as an example
of the way in which the lack of money can obstruct a career by
depriving it of the publicity it needs in an overcrowded market.
The specific comment on literary work is generalised into a point
about work as a whole: "the poor man is a man labouring in
fetters". At the same time, he begins to give Marian some account
of himself. like Reardon he is poor and lacks "the diplomatic
character", but he has no intention of letting this limit him: "I
mean to succeed, you know. I feel that I am one of the men who
do succeed." He will succeed because, in the first place, he offers
a rational account of his own working life ("Literature nowadays
is a trade" [I]), and secondly because he has adapting energies.
These emerge in the mild flirtation he carries on with Marian.
He has let slip Reardon's name accidentally and says "how boy-
ish it was, wasn't it?" and quotes his father's comment on his
tactlessness. Then he asks Marian to indulge him "in a piece of
childishness" which is to watch the London express pass under
the bridge on which they are standing. The invasion of the pastoral
quiet brings an excitement they momentarily share, until Jasper
imposes a meaning on it: "It enspirits me. It makes me feel eager
to go back and plunge into the fight again." Marian replies that

"on me it has just the opposite effect" which Milvain explains by telling her that she just hasn't had enough holiday yet. Then he goes on to link the train with his youth: "It was by a train like that that I first went up to London." Shortly after, they meet Marian's father who clearly belies Jasper's patronising rationalisation of Marian's distaste for the train's meaning, and the following chapter takes us to London and to the home of Milvain's example, Edwin Reardon.

It is a scene which tells us a great deal both about the novel's concern and its method, but what it tells us is mainly in terms of negations. The train, for example, seems to be resonantly significant—its dramatic energy, disrupting the rural quiet, releases a moment of shared excitement, and the authorial adjectives prepare us for Milvain's interpretation: it is impersonal, a "dread force", but the "gleaming rails" and its "volley of sunlit steam" suggest the impersonality of human warfare. And yet whatever metaphoric function it might have is entirely given to it by Jasper who has looked at his watch and timed the intrusion. That is partly why Marian cannot share the excitement beyond the point of its rationalisation. For it is in the end an assimilated phenomenon, with its predictable timetable, its known destination. Trains appear later in the novel but only for what they are, instruments of urban mobility. Reardon will take a train to the East of London when he makes his most decisive move to get out of the literary profession. And when he "becomes practical", that is when he goes to the death that is all he is fit for, he will take a train out of London, but the train reveals nothing, changes nothing. It is not the train of *Dombey and Son*. When Reardon walks away from the closed door of his estranged wife in respectable Westbourne Park, he bumps into Milvain who innocently asks whether he will take a train back to Islington. Reardon walks because he is no longer part of the struggle to survive. Here, in this first passage, Milvain produces the train as an image of his youthful determination—it is a regular event, not new for the new man, but part of the environment in which he makes his way: "I shall go this afternoon by the 2.45", he tells his mother later in the chapter, and it normalises and assimilates what has seemed potentiality an aesthetic revelation. "Safe in the corner of his third class carriage," the last sentence reads, "he smiled at the last glimpse of the familiar fields, and began to think of something he had decided to write for *The West End*." The train images the fight, it brings back the youth of the new man, but the new man rides "safe" within its power.

Milvain gives the train meaning, partly because it is the London express. The chapter is entitled "Holiday"—holidays are functions of urban mobility—the gleaming rail is the line back to the city. New Grub Street is as much a novel of urbanisation as *The Nether World*, and the only ways out of London that are not on a return ticket are the ways taken by Reardon when he goes to his death, Biffen when he walks to Putney Heath to commit suicide, and finally Marian who gets out of the process of literary production by becoming (ironically enough) a provincial librarian. But to speak of the urbanisation of literary production is not the same as speaking of the writer in the city, as though we meant simply an extension of his vision. It is rather the structuring of a labour process and a circulation process in an urban space. The writer's London, the traditional aesthetic perspective is invoked at the opening of the fourth chapter when Gissing describes the view from Reardon's flat roof:

> The green ridge from Hampstead to Highgate, with Primrose Hill and the foliage of Regents Park in the foreground; the suburban spaces of St. John's Wood, Maida Vale, Kilburn; Westminster Abbey and the Houses of Parliament, lying low by the side of the hidden river, and a glassy gleam on far off hills which meant the Crystal Palace; then the clouded majesty of eastern London, crowned by St. Paul's dome. These things one's friends were expected to admire.

The names here are invoked almost epically as T. S. Eliot is later to do, and the panorama is carefully distanced, but the last sentence places this aesthetic vision as a social grace rather than as a meaningful experience. "Living at the very top" of a respectable apartment house, as Reardon does, is an index of poverty, and it is also, of course, the conventional garret of the writer. But the romantic potential of that position is drained out of it, the panorama invoked only to be dismissed. Reardon actually works in a room whose windows overlook the backs of houses skirting Regent's Park—his vision, in this sense, is confined to fragmentary glimpses of a wealthy life from which he is cut off. The "rich glow" from the Western sky that he can also see is only because it is reflected in the higher windows of those houses.

The "actual" London of the novel has none of this potential for aesthetic excitement or moral judgement. Although the writer is not zoned like the factory worker, the nature of the literary market still regionalises the novel. Naturally enough, the characters tend to find themselves lodgings within reach of the British Museum—St. Paul's Crescent, the home of the Yules, is off Camden Road; Jasper Milvain lives in Mornington Road which lay to the East of Regent's Park; and Harold Biffen lives in the poor West End area between Portland Place and Tottenham Court Road. But what is more important than the topographical region is the social zoning which commits the writer to living in a middle-class style on a working-class income. What is striking about the places people live in, in this novel, is their obscurity. Marian, for example, waits for a bus at the end of Tottenham Court Road to take her to "the remoter part of Camden Town" and has to walk ten minutes at the other end of her journey to arrive at "a quiet by-way" (VII). Biffen lives in "a thoroughfare discoverable in the dim district which lies between Portland Place and Tottenham Court Road" (XV). They live in named streets, but streets which are remote or dim. The great thoroughfares, Euston Road, Tottenham Court Road, Camden Road, Hampstead Road, are invoked in the novel as places where people meet or eat or travel in before being absorbed into that charted obscurity. The second point about the working London of the writer is its drab decency. "No one would contest the respectability of the abode" where the Reardons live. (IV); the street where the Yules live consists of "small, decent houses" (VII); Whelpdale lodges at the top of a "house of decent exterior" (XV). And if we compare the names in the novel with the reality recorded in Booth, we find him stressing the decency and respectability of the zones inhabited by these characters. St. Paul's Crescent, for example, is in a zone described as "a fairly respectable block, containing many railway servants, artisans and clerks, and some shop assistants" (Booth II, Appendix, p. 15). Mornington Road is in an area containing "many respectable people finding employment as piano makers, clerks, warehousemen, shop assistants, policemen and kindred trades" (ibid., 14), and Clipstone Street, though it lodges the desperately poor Biffen, is in an area with "only a very small proportion of the poor, mixed with a fair number of artisans in comfortable circumstances" (*ibid*, p. 11). What is also noticeable, of course, in these passages from Booth, is that these areas contain social boundaries. It is neither working-class London nor middle-class London that the writer inhabits, but something poised between the labour aristocracy and the lower middle-class. There is another, more precisely stratified London in the novel: Reardon goes to live among the "working-class of ordinary character" (Booth *loc. cit.*, p. 21) when he moves to Upper Street, and Mrs. Yule's relatives threaten her husband's precarious respectability from Holloway. On the other side of the city, the Carters live in Bayswater and Amy's mother in Westbourne Park, both neighbourhoods of prosperity and middle-class solidity. This non-literary London stresses the social ambiguity of the writer who has to insert himself not among his audience, nor even among his subjects, but among the mobile, shifting world of craftsmen and middle-class hirelings. When Biffen begins to describe his own theory of fiction, which will concern itself with the everyday absurdities of the ignobly decent, Reardon begins to laugh. Harold sharply replies that by laughing Reardon is "taking the side of a cruel omnipotence" (X). What is ironic about this is that it is precisely that laughable, remote, ordinary struggling world that is the London of the literary producer: Jasper and Marian working out their relationship choking on the fog of the Tottenham Court Road, Reardon and Amy breaking up over the choice between increasing poverty and the relative indignity of earning a weekly wage, Alfred Yule having to listen to the rambling complaints of Mrs. Goby—these are ridiculous and "fateful" matters. The aesthetic of *Mr. Bailey, Grocer* is the actuality of the writer's environment. Late in the novel, Reardon laments the fatal attraction of London to the aspiring writer, and says that there is no need for him to live there, unless he wants to make it the subject of his novel. But London is the site of the literary market, and the market rests on a self-generating process of criticism, reviews, in-fighting and publicity. Milvain is all over London—Wimbledon, Westbourne Park, Bloomsbury—fighting to make his mark. And the mark offered to the writer is his secure insertion into the middle-class for whom he writes. He lives in the obscure by-ways on the edge of that insertion. London is not an experience, it is a terrain of struggle, a social space at once neutral and embracing.

As the train is assimilated because it carries us to a known domain, it is also more assimilated by the way in which Milvain links it with his childhood. It shatters the rural air, but it is not, like the train of *Dombey and Son*, an image of change. It does not terrify the present with a sense of time, but rather confirms that present by evoking memories. The metaphor of human warfare confirms this normalisation. Jasper can be nostalgic about the express because he is "a man of his day" for whom the violent machine is part of his essential life, and because his conception of life (exactly what constitutes his modernity) is based on warfare—the train makes him eager to plunge into the fight again. The opening chapter of the novel, over which he presides, is precisely located in 1882, and in every detail he announces a new world. Cracking his boiled egg and announcing a better way to make coffee, he reads his newspaper. The newspaper, like the train, is an instrument of urban mobility; both belong to the realm of communications, at once conquering space and preserving distances (later Jasper will talk about "telegraphic communication"), which is an even more modern system of spatial conquest. Exploiting the objectifying realism of the newspaper, he entertains the breakfast table with the revelation that at that very moment a man is being hanged. It comforts him to know that someone is worse off than himself, and, at the same time, he envies the man who can bring society to its last resource. It is modern because it uses the urban system of communication to turn misery into a commodity; knowing a man is to be hanged is an asset both to comfort and energise oneself. The apparent turnabout (which Milvain accomplishes when, having defended literature to John Yule, he decides to make the latter's attack the basis of an article) is related to a specific form of consistency—the evaluation of actions and attitudes in terms of their effectiveness. And what is effective is what leads to success. Success means seeing the social world as a given environment to which one has to adapt. When he says "I am a stronger man than Reardon" (I), Milvain means precisely this. As we have seen, he is not complacent or acquiescent. When he says that the poor man labours in fetters, he offers a perspective for the whole novel. Nor is he unscrupulous: "One does not like to do brutal things unless one has to you know" (III). But decency is a civilised luxury, one of the rewards of success for Milvain.

Two points need to be stressed about Milvain's "modern" outlook. First, it is based on a self-conscious rationality. Later in the novel, talking to his sisters about his relationship with Marian, he says: "We are both intellectual people, and we talk in an intellectual way. You seem to have rather old-fashioned ideas—provincial ideas (XXIII). "Intellectual" is identified as modern and metropolitan, and it implies "the scientific spirit" (*ibid.*). Talking with Whelpdale, he rejects the word "love" and substitutes for it "fitness" and "compatibility". Marriage, for Milvain, is merely the result of a sentimental conviction that it is possible to find the right woman: "an *educated* man mustn't play so into the hands of ironic destiny" (XXII, my italics). Later, discoursing as he so often does about the realities of literary production, he says that "the struggle for existence among books is nowadays as severe as among men" (XXXIII). Milvain's rationality is that of social Darwinism—the application of the scientific spirit to social organisation. At the end of the novel, Marian precisely compliments him as an exemplar of the rationality: Milvain has been contrasting his luck with that of his fallen "companions", Reardon and Biffen:

> "You are better fitted to fight your way, Jasper."
> "More of a brute, you mean."
> "You know very well I don't. You have more energy and more intellect." (XXXVI)

Being a "brute" is not what constitutes the man of his day: the fit man has energy and intellect. And this leads to the second point that needs stressing. Being strong does not mean being anything of a superman—it means adapting, remaining inside apart from yourself. Whenever Milvain talks about his writing, he is fully aware that he writes rubbish, just as he knows that the social structure he plays is iniquitous. Strength in this novel is not a heroic privilege, it is rather available to the rational mind. It is not for nothing that Jasper spends so much time trying to sort out Reardon's problems—Reardon's retreat into a difference of temperament threatens the intellectual accuracy of the social Darwinist reality. Realism and adaptability define an area of freedom in a highly determined world—it is crucial to our understanding of the novel that we shouldn't just think of Milvain as an appalling cynic.

The more so because his role is complex. Milvain dominates the opening chapters of the novel. Not only does Gissing present him to us as a character, but initiates his relationship with Marian. Both in terms of career and of love Jasper is at the beginning of his own story, and the well worked out attitudes to literature and life which he announces seem to be part of a process of self-definition which has yet to be tried by experience. And yet after this opening he recedes into the background, his only important structural function being that of the lover of Marian, a catalyst in the much more dominant chemistry of her relationship with her father. Then, at the very end of the novel, he is left in the foreground, filling the gap left by Reardon. In the middle, he acts mainly as commentator on other characters, occasionally giving an account of his own progress in brisk statements about his routine of work. It is as though Gissing wants us to involve ourselves in the man of his day only to make a mirror image of his opposite, the old type of unpractical artist, and only to become the unresponsive object of Marian's pent-up joy. The combination of the sense of beginning with a sense of articulated values leads us to expect a conflict which never emerges. Marian shares a moment of spontaneous energy with Milvain and breaks away from him when he rationalises it, but she will not be able to challenge that rationality in him because her father and luck will prevent her. Reardon is cited as an example of opposing artistic values, but he does not have the strength or integrity to question the dictum that literature nowadays is a trade.

To say that nothing in the novel opposes Milvain's rationality is to put it too mildly. On the contrary, as we shall see, Reardon's whole story depends on his tacit acquiescence in Milvain's world view. He may lament the making of literature into a trade, but this is not because he has a literary integrity which offers an alternative view. Although he claims to shrink from "conscious insincerity of workmanship", he sees this as an absurd incon-

sistency and admits that he is "no uncompromising artistic ped-
ant" (IV), and confronted with Milvain's commercial attitudes,
he merely comments that the latter is "naturally light hearted
and hopeful" while he is "naturally the opposite". This is linked
with his explicit acceptance of the social Darwinist rationality:
"A man has no business to fail; least of all can he expect others
to look back upon him or pity him if he sink under the stress of
conflict. Those behind will trample over his body; they can't help
it" (XIX)—the only difference between this and Milvain's view lies
in its denial of the area of freedom constituted by that rationality. The same process goes on in Marian's relationship with
Milvain. Her feeling for him is largely a sense of the power be-
queathed on her momentarily by John Yule's money. She wants
passionate love from him but that is because her ego has always
been crushed into submission. Milvain is sexless; only in a
moment of vulgar weakness does he think of Marian outside the
terms of his ambition, and in the end it is Amy who transforms
his view of literary success into a process of sexual selection,
whose mother is a social Darwinian model—"She must crush
or be crushed" (XVIII)—who turns out to be the right woman.
Only Biffen offers anything like an alternative integrity, and his
artistic commitment is, if gently, mocked. Jasper Milvain disappears as protagonist because, however we might be appalled
by his trivialisation of literature, his rationality effectively becomes the novel's reality.

Irving Howe ("Introduction", p. xvii) has termed Gissing "the
poet of fatigue". New Grub Street certainly seems to support
this description. The place of literature in social life is, of course,
a major concern in the nineteenth century, and that is most
obviously what the novel seems to announce itself as being about.
The problem is that if that is its subject, it seems like a peculi-
arly defeatist treatment of it: defeatist and unrepresentative,
even in terms of Gissing's own career. Set in the early 'eighties,
it chooses to ignore a whole dimension of literary history which
certainly opposed the mere incorporation of literature into a
philistine hegemony—I mean the movement which produced
Henry James's "The Art of Fiction", Whistler's "Ten O'Clock
Lecture", George Moore's "Literature at Nurse" and which Gissing
himself participated in effectively enough to earn the soubriquet

"Gissing the Rod" from *Punch*. James's novel of 1891, *The Tragic Muse*, for all its scepticism, has much more sense of the oppositional potential of aesthetic integrity than *New Grub Street*. And in larger terms, Gissing's novel seems to be a fatigued contribution to the debate about culture and society which embraces literary history from Arnold to Williams. It is true that the novel registers certain specific developments which had major cultural significance[2]—the rise of the literary agent, the coming of new kinds of publishers like Jedwood who would experiment with ways of finding larger markets, popular journalism like Whelpdale's *Chit Chat*, but there is no overwhelming sense of a mass culture because there is very little sense of the reading public. Amy Reardon is the nearest we have to a portrayal of a reader, and she becomes attached to the relatively specific developments in higher journalism, and Amy is too much involved with literary production to have anything but contempt for the sentimentalities of popular fiction. But what is most important is that the market is a given reality which is never questioned. It is noticeable that Milvain doesn't criticise Reardon for the kind of things he writes; what he attacks is the way he deals with his work.

If the novel seems to engage with the problem of the cultural changes brought about by the development of literature in relation to mass literacy in a very marginal way, it is partly because it so focusses on the process of production. Literature is never fully represented as a mode of social communication. At the same time, so much of the novel is taken up not with the specific issue of literature, but with a much more general theme, that of success and failure, that we have to ask ourselves whether it is really concerned with the role of literature in society, or whether that is merely a specific form of the nature of survival in a Darwinian social world. The word which divides Milvain and Reardon is "practical". It occurs again and again in the novel, sometimes ironically (as in the title of the chapter in which Reardon dies—"Reardon Becomes Practical"), sometimes with a more urgent relevance. To be practical or not practical is not an index of artistic worth or cultural rightness. But it is at the centre of a specific group of questions about the social career of the writer. When Reardon, late in the novel, laments the success of certain writers, Harold Biffen replies "What does it matter? We are different types of intellectual workers . . . Their work answers a demand; ours . . . doesn't" (XXVII). The poor man is a man labouring in fetters—*New Grub Street* is very much a trade novel, not about mass culture, but about work, the conditions and remuneration of work. Its proper context is specific, and if we attend to that context we shall be in a better position to judge whether the only value opposing success in the market is fatigue. We shall find that the novel has large significances, but at the moment we have to say that it is a novel about the payment of the writer. Its apparent capitulation to the social Darwinism which is ideologically deplored results from this. Just as it is not the writer's London but the London in which the writer works, so too it is not the debasement of literature in the market, but the struggle of the literary producer to secure himself a living, that is the question of *New Grub Street*.

2

She kept asking herself what was the use and purpose of such a life as she was condemned to lead. When already there was more good literature in the world than any mortal could cope with in his lifetime, here she was exhausting herself in the manufacture of printed stuff which no one even pretended to be more than a commodity for the day's market. What unspeakable folly! To write—was not that the joy and privilege of one who had an urgent message for the world? Her father, she knew well, had no such message: he had abandoned all thought of original production, and only wrote about writing. She herself would throw away her pen with joy but for the need of earning money. And all these people about her, what aim had they save to make new books out of those already existing, that yet newer books might in turn be made out of theirs? This huge library, growing into unwieldiness, threatening to become a trackless desert of print—how intolerably it weighed upon the spirit! (VIII)

Marian's question, which is the broadest version of the novel's question, is put when she is exhausted by the work she is condemned to, and it is put in the place of work, realised as a material environment, the radial reading room of the British Museum, which in this moment of exhausted pause impinges itself on Marian's mind as a rapid series of images—limbo ("an eternity of vain research along endless shelves"), a huge web, a prison shaped like Bentham's panopticon. Images of compulsion, the library which should emancipate us from ignorance, as the factory should emancipate us from material deprivation, only condemning us to darkness. She puts the question in terms of the alienating effect of capitalism—the contradiction between use-value and exchange-value ("commodity"), and like a worker locked in a labour process which can have no meaning (since one's work, seen in its broadest perspective, is not for someone but for an abstraction, the market). The British Museum is exactly the workplace of the capitalised literary producer, and although the writer is strictly speaking self-employed, the social geography of literary production—a symbolic space that, whatever its primal intentions, pays tribute to the market—mirrors in its architecture the endless circuits of oppression of the urbanised worker. At the same time, the recollection of the "true" function of writing, the communication of an "urgent message for the world", is phrased as an almost naïve nostalgia: it is as though this writer can only conceive of the use-value of writing as an empty phrase, something that is not experienced, merely known about.

The title of the novel keeps the question posed within specific limits. Grub Street is a term which comes into full significance when the writer becomes committed to the market. Milvain says that Reardon handles his books as though he were living in Sam Johnson's Grub Street (I); Reardon himself admits that the writer is drawn to London because he forms his ideas "from old literature" and goes on to say "we think and talk like Chatterton" (XXXI). These allusions to a more congenial past are still within the terms of a market economy, and earlier, when Reardon enviously recalls Coleridge's benefactor, James Gillman, he is not harking back to a system of patronage, but simply to an easing of the conditions within which the writer has to make a living. Alfred Yule recalls that the word "literature" itself, with its special meaning, comes into being only after writing has become committed to the market. In other words, when Jasper says that literature nowadays is a trade, he is not saying something that it hasn't always been—the three invoked writers all knew what it meant to have to try to obtain enough payment. "Old literature", the better time, merely means that literature produced when the market wasn't too complicated for an "unpractical artist" to survive in (though survival is a relative term given Johnson's poverty and Chatterton's suicide). The novel does not look beyond a situation when there is no conflict between the urgent message and the day's market. What is new about Gissing's Grub Street is that the message has been lost altogether in the struggle to keep the writer alive.

The major text that has most obvious bearing on this specific concern is Carlyle's "The Hero as Man of Letters" (1840). Carlyle is not writing about writers in general (there is another lecture on the hero as poet) but about a specifically modern phenomenon, "a product of these new ages", unknown before the eighteenth century, the result of the democratic triumph of print: "Never, till about a hundred years ago, was there seen any figure of a Great Soul living apart in that anomalous manner; endeavouring to speak forth the inspiration that was in him by Printed Books." It is anomalous because the relationship between the hero and his beneficiaries is mediated by an object which is for sale in the marketplace: "much had been sold and bought, and left to make its own bargain in the marketplace; but the inspired wisdom of a Heroic Soul never till then in that naked manner". That wisdom is, of course, in Carlyle's Germanic romantic vocabulary, The Divine Idea which is unrecognisable in the world to the "mass of men" who live "among the superficialities, practicalities and shows of the world". The Man of Letters differs from the poet in that he has to make this Divine Idea prevail within the practicalities and shows of the world, has to find "place and subsistence by what the world would please to give him for doing that". The anomaly, what later Carlyle terms with resonant accuracy "the anomaly of a disorganic literary class", is essential to what the Man of Letters is, an accident in society, who wanders "like a wild Ishmaelite, in a world of which he is the spiritual light, either the guidance or the misguidance". Not surprisingly, Carlyle's first example of the hero as man of letters is Dr. Johnson (and the last is the mate of Chatterton in Wordsworth's stanza about the youth and despondency of poets in "Resolution and Independence"—Burns), and, unlike other kinds of hero, the man of letters is not a conqueror but one who "fought bravely and fell".

The inevitable anomaly in Carlyle is heroic because what matches his interest in the conditions of production is an idealist mystification of writing. Writing is the urgent message of the Divine Idea, and thus, although the writer is an outsider precisely because he is at the mercy of the market, his fate is a significant index of society: "the world's manner of treating him is the most significant feature of the world's general position". The disorganic position of the writer is dialectically opposed to his organic centrality in man's activity. For everything that man does is but an image of his thought:

> For indeed, whatever be the outward form of the thing (bits of paper, as we say, and black ink), is it not verily, at bottom, the highest act of man's faculty that produces a Book? It is the *Thought* of man; the true thaumaturgic virtue, by which man works all things whatsoever. All that he does, and brings to pass, is the vesture of a Thought. This London City, with all its houses, palaces, steam engines, cathedrals, and huge immeasurable traffic and tumult, what is it but a Thought, but millions of Thoughts made into One; a huge immeasurable Spirit of a THOUGHT, embodied in brick, in iron, smoke, dust, Palaces, Parliaments, Hackney Coaches, Katherine Docks, and the rest of it! Not a brick was made but some man had to think of the making of that brick.—The thing we called "bits of paper with traces of black ink", is the *purest* embodiment a Thought of man can have. No wonder it is, in all ways, the activest and noblest.

We mustn't be mislead by the breathless rhetoric into thinking that Carlyle is idiosyncratic. It is merely a reformulation of the romantic image of the artist, and it is, of course, precisely when that image is being most fully worked out, when the poet is defined as prophet and legislator in different ways, that his insertion into the market is being worked out as well. But Carlyle's affirmation here clearly supplies a rationale for Dickens's excited reproduction of what he sees in London too. It enables us to define very precisely what goes on in *New Grub Street*. For Gissing's London is not millions of thoughts made into one: it is neither organic, since it is structured as a system of distances, nor human, since it is a reified, neutral environment. For Carlyle there is a strictly balanced dialectic: if the man of letters has to descend into the marketplace, what he sells there is the purest embodiment of all other creations of men, so that in reflecting the age, the age reflects him. Poverty and failure (in worldly terms) can therefore be instructive for the man of letters, and since the problem of remuneration is anomalous, it can be accepted as something insoluble. For Carlyle, the worst element of the life of his literary heroes is that "they found their business and position such a chaos". For Gissing, in some ways, that is the only element: for New Grub Street, the disorganic literary class is entirely secularised. There is no Divine Idea by which the anomaly can be overturned.

Carlyle chooses to write about Dr. Johnson because he is the first major author to be a true man of letters with a total commitment to the market. Leslie Stephen in 1876 described Johnson as "not the first professional author . . . but perhaps the first man who made the profession respectable"[3] and, of course, he cites Johnson's famous dictum that no man but a blockhead ever wrote except for money. Johnson is thus available as an example for those who want to argue that literature can be inserted into society like any trade or profession:

> An author was, according to him, a man who turned out books as a bricklayer turns out houses or a tailor coats. So long as he supplied a good article and got a fair price, he was a fool to grumble, and a humbug to affect loftier motives.
>
> (Ibid.)

But Stephen is careful to place this attitude in its proper context —a contempt for amateurs and patrons—and he devotes much of his chapter to describing the difficulty eighteenth-century writers had in making a living out of authorship, but what is important is that he can conceive of Johnson's writing in terms of a career. In the same year that New Grub Street was published, Sir Walter Besant[4] wrote an assessment of Johnson's career, "Over Johnson's Grave", in which he claims first that he was a "bookseller's hack" and remained so all his life, "in the sense that he lived by finding out subjects which the public may be supposed to like, and writing on those subjects" (1903, pp. 263–64); and second that he was a modestly prosperous hack who "with no family connections at all to help him, no degree, and no money, did, in adopting the profession of literature, better for himself than if he had taken orders, gone to the bar, become a physician, or remained a schoolmaster" (*ibid.*, p. 268). This seems to be a resolution of Carlyle's anomaly by a total inversion of the Divine Idea in the market place, and indeed Gissing thought of Besant as one who had done much in his own time to bring about the commercialisation of literature. But the contrast between Besant and Carlyle goes deeper than this. Carlyle speaks of a disorganic literary *class*, and Besant in an essay of 1889 refers to Carlyle's involvement in the Society of British Authors founded in 1843. This was according to Besant an abortive attempt on the part of writers to form an activist group. It failed, he says, because it tried to work on an impossible theory that writing is a single profession which can be organised as a guild with its own professional etiquette, whereas it is "at the most a collection of professions". And he goes on to affirm that: "There is one thing, and one thing only, for which those who write books and papers which are sold can possibly unite—viz., their material interests" (*ibid.*, p. 281). The class is thus to be identified by its insertion into the market, that is what constitutes its group dynamic. If *New Grub Street* registers a secularisation of the man of letters, it is in response to a specific development, of which Besant, on the face of it, is representative. For precisely in the year in which the novel is mainly set, Besant was the major driving force behind the founding of the modern Society of Authors, which, as he points out, rectified in its practice the naïveté of the British Society of 1843.

Besant is an important figure for Gissing and for *New Grub Street* particularly. Although he was an older man, his career is entangled with Gissing's in several ways. Besant regarded himself as the heir of the great popular novelists of the mid-century, especially Dickens. He began his career as a solo novelist in the early eighties, like Gissing, and, at precisely the same time that Gissing was beginning to write about the London proletariat, wrote *All Sorts and Conditions of Men* and *The Children of Gibeon*, both of which dealt with the same subject, and in fact, both writers were discussed comparatively in a long review in

Frasers Magazine of 1888, "Two Philanthropic Novelists" by Edith Sichel. The links are ironic, because Gissing and Besant are in every way opposed to one another—Besant is a sentimental and moralistic writer who sees the novel as a vast engine of popular reform, and his novels sold extremely well. He is a kind of mirror image of Gissing and it is not surprising that his review of *New Grub Street* should, on the face of it, misunderstand the novel. He discusses Reardon with total contempt: "He has no education to speak of; he has no knowledge of society; he has no personal experiences: he has no travel . . . It is not possible for such a man to succeed"; and he speaks of Milvain with complete respect: "his career illustrates the advantages to be derived from accepting the existing conditions, and trading upon them" (*The Critical Heritage*, pp. 181–82). Although there is obvious filtering in this (one of Reardon's troubles is that travel has made him dissatisfied), the terms in which Besant does it are precisely those terms established by Milvain—adaptation and success. In what might have been a further comment on the novel, Besant was to write in 1892, in "The Literary Career":

> The world loves the successful man because he commands their love. He touches their hearts. Therefore while they despise the helpless, dependent, the uncertain, unpractical trade of letters, they love the man of letters who can move them.
>
> (1903, p. 335)

For Carlyle the man of letters is the Ishmaelitish hero in the market place, for Besant he is a hero of the market place. But Besant, more than anybody else in the eighteen eighties, is concerned with literature as a career—he offers the Darwinian norm on which the novel is built.

But it is not so simple. The marketing of literature is no more a "real" representation of the social relations of literary production than the marketing of commodities in general is a real reflection of the social relations of production. And Besant is a writer whose ideology unconsciously reveals the unreality of this secularisation. If Carlyle mystifies literature with the divine idea, the "practical" attitude to literature has to borrow that mystification for its ultimate ratification. We can see this most clearly in Besant's own novel about the literary career, *All in A Garden Fair*, published in the year of *New Grub Street*'s setting, 1883. As in Gissing's novel, the literary life is bound up with the general question of economic survival, which in turn is linked to sexual selection. It is the story of three young men in love with one girl who is the daughter of an exiled republican of 1848, Hector Philippon. They are brought up in a village near London whose mature population is dominated by a group of prosperous bankrupts from the City. One of the young men enters trade while the other two, Allen and Will, start careers as City merchants. Allen, however, encouraged by Hector, develops literary propensities and, with the radical exile teaching him to regard the role of the writer as the voice of the people, decides instead to become a novelist. The question that dominates the plot is what choice the daughter will make. The man in trade becomes entangled in fraud; Will goes off to China on business for most of the story. But although Hector and Claire spend most of their time assuming that Allen will be the man, and therefore concerning themselves with his career, it is Will, back from Shanghai with an adequate supply of social awareness and financial security, who carries off the prize to a life of philanthropic bliss. Allen meanwhile marries a bluestocking who can do justice to his work by reading it to enthralled audiences.

The most obvious interest of the novel is that despite its apparently radical conception of art as the voice of the people, Allen's career is portrayed in Milvainic terms. Once in London, Allen is taught to look on his profession in a practical and optimistic way:

> "There is so much to do in literature," said his advisor, "that the difficulty is to find out what you can do best, and what will pay you best. The world is continually crying out for new books, for instance: not books which take up half a man's lifetime and advance things; books to be read and tossed aside; light books, tales, novels."
>
> (188, II, 103)

This is said without cynicism, and when Allen protests that he does not want to be a mere book-maker, his advisor reminds him of the example of Johnson and launches into a celebration of the possibilities with an enthusiasm comparable to the peripatetic moment of a Hollywood musical ("all the newspapers to be kept going . . ."). Allen's career begins when he gets the editorship of the organ of the leather trade, and he works up from this by writing for the magazines (beginning with a chatty piece about a picturesque French poet) and then by sending in the manuscript of a story set up as proofs to fool an editor into thinking he had already accepted it. After that, Allen has no trouble in becoming a popular novelist and playwright. Like Milvain, he trades on circumstances, and the novel is refreshingly honest about how important social success is among these circumstances:

> "But you have always been preaching that no one can help a writer."
> "No one can in his writing; but people can talk about him when he has begun to write. Don't you see? They can force a man."
>
> (*Ibid.*, II, 171)

As Milvain says: "Men won't succeed in literature that they may get into society, but will get into society that they may succeed in literature" (III). Allen's career is undoubtedly romanticised, but what it romanticises is the "reality" of success.

But if the central volume is concerned with the material conditions of the literary career in this way, the first volume, which is taken up with the preparation of Allen to undertake this career, relies on a very different kind of idealisation. Hector teaches Allen to regard literature as a sacred office: the poet leads the people and is the interpreter of their thought. Allen is sent not merely to study art, but also to go into the poor quarters of London (which, like the London of *The Nether World*, is a version of Dante's Hell) to find the voice of the people, so that he can lead them via a bloodless and undemocratic revolution to fulfil human destiny (which is to be happy). Hector is noble but unrealistic, and that is why it is Will, the practical man of business who does not get carried away by rhetoric, who turns out to be the real leader of men. Nevertheless, this education remains the basis of Allen's art: among the faces in the crowd, he sees a girl's and she becomes a muse to him, It is in trying to imagine her story that Allen finds the material for his first novel. Thus though the literary career is frankly secularised and presented as a mixture of opportunism, drudgery, luck and good contacts, the process of writing is highly mystified. Possessed by the young girl's image, he writes his novel "in a kind of rapture" (*ibid.*, III, 310). Although the literary career can be rationalised in terms of the market, the commodity by whose sale it survives has to be produced in a mystic aura: "happy is he who is possessed by a story" (II, 306).

Besant is not as naïve as this account would suggest. The third volume seems to engage with the fundamental ambiguity in a way which reveals an unease that can only be accommodated by a kind of jocular worldly wisdom in the tone. For all that it is a face from the people that has inspired Allen, he becomes totally indifferent to their actual lives except insofar that he finds there material for his art. Supposedly the first novelist "to portray a mean life" (II, 312), he is the wrong man for Hector's revolution because art is "A beautiful sorceress" (II, 122) and through his art, as Claire realises, he has come to "dwell in the unreal" (III, 140). Allen marries into the aesthetic élite to whom any threat of equality is anathema. He does not betray his principles, but he does retreat into his nature, and we are made to feel that he is lucky both because he is inspired and because he is protected by a circle which venerates and activates his inspiration. The third volume could easily become a very bitter satire of the mid-Victorian confidence in the social efficacy and acceptability of art, and it only doesn't because Besant is committed to a double standard. Literature is in the first place a rational career structure: the only thing which obstructs success is the inequity inherent in publishing (which can be changed by writers becoming more practical as a body of men). On the other hand, it is a mystery based on talent which may not be recognised outside an informed élite. Hence also, in the 'eighties, Besant is arguing for an academy to operate the standards of that mystery. It is interesting to note both in "The Literary Career" and in his *Autobiography* that Besant advocates becoming independent before turning to writing fiction. For someone who professed confidence in the rationality of the market and the popular acclaim of works of art, this seems remarkable. It also is of particular relevance to *New Grub Street*, as we shall see. For the moment it is important to stress that for Besant, the most articulate "real" spokesman of the Milvainic view of literature in the 'eighties, the most reliable explanation of why men pursue it as a profession is that "by nature" writing is "a continual joy" to them, and that it is "an exercise of force" (1903, p. 334).

What in Besant is glaringly evident as an unconfronted contradiction is, in Gissing, a hopeless anomaly—trying to make the imagination (which is a mystified concept central to bourgeois aesthetics) pay for one's living. The paradox is that if you deny the imagination, you strip away the mystified aura which surrounds the writer's commodity. Reardon is not merely faced with an unappreciative public, he is also faced with the drying up of his imagination. He hasn't Allen's luck in that sense either. Milvain can only survive because he can shelter behind this aura, make his audience feel that he is not what he is. There is no way of accounting for this anomaly rationally within the terms of the bourgeois ideology, except in a way that exposes that ideology as ideological. Besant argued again and again that the novel was the most popular form and that it was an engine of reform, but towards the end of his career he makes a very different kind of point:

> The novelist, unconsciously perhaps, writes for a class. Principally he writes for the middle class to which he generally belongs: he writes for them because they are the largest class of readers, and because he knows their ideas, and their views of life.
>
> (1899, p. 111)

That is explicitly the crucial issue of *All in A Garden Fair*—the writer finds the voice of the people, but it is as a mode of insertion into a class, which is why, almost inevitably, art becomes indifferent to the life which informs it. That is what precisely constitutes the mystic aura of the commodity. The Society of Authors, whose chief propagandist Besant was, treated the writer's product as "property". But what constitutes the value of the commodity is the labour which has gone into the making of it, and there is no way in which the writer can be remunerated directly for this labour in a market economy. His special anomaly is that he has to produce the commodity and is only paid insofar as he can lay claim to owning it. That is why, almost inevitably, he has to belong to the middle class— so that he can establish those rights of ownership. But he is also a worker—he has nothing but his labour to sell—and it is the publisher who turns that labour into a marketable commodity. So that it is not merely a cultural anomaly which makes the novel a middle-class form— it is a function of its mode of insertion into the general social relations of production (the novel is more vulnerable than other literary forms to this contradiction because it is the form most directly linked, from its beginning, to the commitment of literature to the market). Therefore the writer is a special form of social unclassifiability, as Carlyle with startling clarity realised:

> . . . this wild welter of a chaos which is called Literary Life: this too is a kind of ordeal! There is clear truth in the idea that a struggle from the lower class of society towards the upper regions and rewards of society, must ever continue. Strong men are born there, who ought to stand elsewhere than there. The manifold, inextricably complex universal struggle of these constitutes, and must constitute, what is called the progress of society. For Men of Letters, as for all other sorts of men. How to regulate that struggle? There is the whole question.

Milvain doesn't have this kind of problem exactly, because he is content at his stage to be an intellectual worker, simply producing goods required for magazines. By being a good literary clerk he will survive and make his way into the middle class. But for Reardon, Biffen, Yule, Whelpdale and the others who have to market their labour, there is an insoluble anomaly—to reduce imagination, which has an aura of property, to the level of work, or to market that work as though it possessed that aura for which the middle class treasure the literary commodity. Besant's answer is to make yourself a member of the middle class by good journey-work first. But it makes nonsense of the rationality of the market. The literary career is a special form of the confrontation between labour and capital, because it is a confrontation which goes on within the writer's individual situation. Self-employed, and yet labouring in fetters, his failure exposes the necessity of that conflict.

Marian's feeling that it is the very "joy and privilege" of literary work which is denied by the form which her own labour takes is thus not merely a function of her personal disillusion. It is no accident that she longs by comparison for manual work and that Reardon resolves his predicament by becoming a "decent wage-earner". For the special twist of the fate of the literary producer is that the market at once precludes the urgent message and demands it in fetishised form in the aura of inspiration or intellectual distinction for which it pays. The structure of the novel cannot base itself on a conflict of values, because that would fail to register the double determination of the demand on the writer. On the contrary, Gissing has to find a structure which will register at once the effect of this on the personal identity of the writer, and situate his predicament as the member of a class. Because it is a disorganic class, he has to portray total isolation of the individual producer in relation to the group membership which determines the impossibility of that individual's freedom.

3

The structure of *New Grub Street* is based on a common convention of Victorian fiction, which is to have two interwoven stories which in terms of narrative are largely independent of one another but which echo and contrast, thus creating a double effect of panorama and unity. Until Reardon's death in chapter XXXII, there are ten episodes which alternate between what is essentially Marian's story on the one hand and Reardon's on the other. These episodes overlap very often in time, so that there is an effect of taking one story up to a given point and going back to take up the other. The novel is often discussed as though the Reardon story was the main plot, but this is not true at least in terms of the space devoted to each, and given that Marian's story opens the novel and goes on after the Reardon story is finished. The interaction of these stories is, however, different from the interaction of the two plots of, say, Eliot's *Middlemarch* in which the stories of Lydgate and Dorothea mutually enforce one another's meaning. In *New Grub Street*, the effect is rather that of the stories neutralising each other, making each experience relative by the sense that what we learn in one is undercut by the other. Additionally, neither of the plots are worked out—they

131

simply disintegrate. Reardon becomes the spectator of his own drama (XXV) and so merely drifts towards death, and Marian is visited by a double "catastrophe" (a notably theatrical term) which merely leaves her more inexorably trapped in the situation she is in at the beginning. As happens so often in Gissing, the conventions of the Victorian novel seem to be used to create expectancies in the reader which are sardonically frustrated.

The co-existence of the two stories insists on the group pattern, but the way in which they reflect each other emphasises the isolation of the protagonist. For what happens to Marian ironically comments on Reardon's suffering without informing it or enabling us to bring to bear a larger perspective: the perspective is just different. Reardon is trapped within the market conditions of his profession, Marian within the system of institutions, literature as a process of learning which generates part of that market, though not a part that Reardon exploits. Reardon's retreat is into the scholasticism which keeps Marian tied to the British Museum—the destructive nature of the commercialisation of literature is matched by the pedantry and squabbling of literature itself. Equally, on a different level, Reardon's failure is reflected in the failure of his marriage, and this specifically takes the form of jealousy of his child: "He was beginning to dislike the child. But for Willie's existence Amy would still love him with undivided heart" (XII). Marian is oppressed by her father—she is doomed by the relationship Reardon rejects from the other end. Both Reardon and Yule take refuge in self-pity, both are anachronisms and though they are obviously presented with some compassion, it is not insignificant that both Marian and Amy turn to the unself-pitying man of his day as a way out of the traps they are caught in as women. Moreover, if Amy seems harshly hostile to poverty and failure, Marian undergoes the whole process of personal degradation which poverty and failure can bring. Amy is brought to despise romantic love and the novels which enact its ideology, and Marian wants that kind of love from Milvain: nevertheless it is not that she sees him as a great lover, it is just that she wants to experience the joy of command that her apparent legacy brings her. Traditional cultural values—parental respect, marital loyalty—turn sour on the women of the novel and they can only survive by opting out of the relationships which place them. Marian's story ensures that we do not sentimentalise Reardon or dismiss Amy as callous. Equally, Reardon's story makes it difficult to see the confrontation of Marian with her father as a simple opposition of oppressed and oppressor—in their personal relationship they simply act out of the dilemma of the literary class as a whole.

This dilemma is based on the way in which the literary profession has access to money. On the one hand, there is the market in which the writer has to sell his commodity which is what he produces, a book. On the other hand, there is a network of institutions through which the writer can command status and prestige and hence obtain an indirect form of patronage. Reardon has become a novelist because he doesn't want to be a schoolteacher, that is, to be part of an established institution. Yule is a frustrated teacher who has to live by writing books because there is no academy. To escape from the market is to be at the mercy of the institution. Amy marries Reardon partly out of respect for his talent—"you'll be a great man" (V). Later, when she is separated from him, she will turn to serious journalism for the staple of her reading. The open market is deeply bound up with the social patronage available to art from an aspiring élite. Equally, if Yule is committed to the idea of the journal as a way of expressing his pedantry, Marian refuses him the capital because it will not be a good investment. When Amy tells Reardon that "Art must be practised as a trade, at all events in our time. This is the age of trade" (IV), she is echoing only part of Milvain's formula for success which includes going into society, attaining the prestige due to a writer as a precondition of the market. Essentially what we see in the novel as a motivating process is exactly the same as we see in *The Nether World*, a scarcity of money within the group making it necessary to pursue conflicting roads of access, and that is why the dilemma of the writer in his work and the remuneration of his work becomes also a dilemma of his very identity.

For both Reardon and Marian, the ordeal of poverty is an ordeal of sexuality. "Don't you feel it's rather unmanly this state of things? You say you love me, and I try to believe it. But whilst you are saying so, you let me get nearer to miserable, hateful poverty" (III); thus Amy, at the beginning of the novel, equates economic failure with sexual failure. Marian too, is sexually insulted by Jasper as long as he can feel her fingers to be ink stained, and once she has lost her money, she is sexually bereaved. The pattern in her life of repression and illusory emancipation is realised with great sharpness by Gissing—the repression continuing to overshadow the release, the release and its inherent limitations (particularly its dependence on the sexless Milvain) commenting on the smouldering rebellion of the outward conformity—and it comments ironically on Reardon's loss of self-respect. In a sense, he is unmanly to capitulate to poverty. Throughout the discussions with Amy he is continually protesting his weakness and demanding to be loved for that weakness. At the same time, he admires her precisely for her strength: "though slenderly fashioned, she was so gloriously strong" (V). When Amy and Reardon are alienated from one another, he resorts to power games which are both egoistic and feeble: "He hoped to cause her pain equal to his own, for then it would be in his power to throw off this disguise, and soothe her with every soft word his heart could suggest" (XV). Reardon is like Meredith's egoist without the support of wealth—sentimental, devious, self-pitying. At the moment of crisis, when he is face to face with Amy's strength, he feels that he ought to strike her but instead sheds tears. Again and again, Gissing stresses Reardon's passivity:

> A dark fear began to shadow him. In yielding thus passively to stress of circumstance, was he not exposing his wife to a danger which outweighed all the ills of poverty? . . . He knew very well that a man of strong character would never have entertained this project. He had got into the way of thinking of himself as too weak to struggle against the obstacles on which Amy insisted, and of looking for safety in retreat.
>
> (XVII)

Reardon is a self-willed failure to some extent. The kind of judgement he passes on himself here is a retreat into the social Darwinian norms of Milvain—thinking of oneself as too weak to overcome circumstances is not a sign of detachment but of taking comfort in ready made, pseudo-scientific terms like "strong character". In Marian's case, the desexualisation comes from the overlapping of social and sexual selection. In the Museum she feels herself to be a machine not a woman; Jasper gives her her first "taste of life", enables her to confront her father, and in fact to confront Jasper himself when he is trying to wriggle out of the engagement. Marian is more straightforwardly a victim of social realities than Reardon. Reardon is condemned by his acquiescence in the ideology which rejects him.

This explains why it is difficult not to feel impatient with Reardon, why if you didn't know something about Gissing you might, not stupidly, read the novel in something like the way Besant does. Yet, at the same time, Reardon is often taken to be Gissing's exponent character—his self-pity to be Gissing's self-pity. That is why it is so important to stress the double plot. Reardon may have many of Gissing's ideas and more of his complaints about the world at large, but he clearly is not meant as an autobiographical character. The self-pity is obviously there as a crippling aesthetic as well as moral obstacle. Unlike Gissing's novels, Reardon's are said to be lacking "in local colour" (V), and he is not, like Gissing, capable of making art out of the pressure of actuality: "With such terrible real things pressing upon me, my imagination can shape nothing substantial" (IV). If, then, we are not meant to take Reardon as any kind of norm, if his story and suffering is undercut or, to be more precise, made relative by Marian's story, how is Gissing using him? If this is a novel about the anomaly of the inorganic literary class, how can the suffering of a self-willed failure among its members reflect anything of that anomaly?

I have already argued that the fundamental motif of the Gissing novel is the condition of being unclassed, which unlike the declassment of the classical realist novel is not the basis of a privileged protagonist: the Gissing character has no access to typicality. It is only by being a special case that he becomes the register of the contradictions of the economic world which leaves him trapped in the anomalous condition of his group. In *New Grub Street*, Gissing makes Reardon a special case by suddenly stepping out of the novel and challenging the reader:

> The chances are that you have neither understanding nor sympathy for men such as Edwin Reardon and Harold Biffen. They

merely provoke you. They seem to you inert, flabby, weakly envious, foolishly obstinate, impiously mutinous, and many other
things. You are made angrily contemptuous by their failure to
get on; why don't they bestir themselves, push and hustle, welcome kicks so long as halfpence follow, make a place in the
world's eye—in short take a leaf from the book of Mr. Jasper
Milvain?

But try to imagine a personality wholly unfitted for the rough
and tumble of the world's labour market. From the familiar
point of view these men were worthless; view them in possible
relation to a humane order of society, and they are admirable
citizens. Nothing is easier than to condemn a type of character
which is unequal to the coarse demands of life as it suits the
average man. These two were richly endowed with the kindly
and imaginative virtues; if fate threw them amid incongruous
circumstances, is their endowment of less value? You scorn their
passivity; but it was their nature and their merit to be passive.
Gifted with independent means, each of them would have taken
quite a different aspect in your eyes. The sum of their faults was
their inability to earn money; but, indeed, that inability does not
call for unmingled disdain. (XXXI)

It looks as though Gissing is trying to make up for the fact that
he has made Reardon so much less than a cultural hero and so
has to turn on the reader for being too philistine. We notice the
way in which the third sentence gradually accretes a kind of
glamour to Reardon and Biffen—"inert, flabby, weakly envious"
is very different from "impiously mutinous". At the same time,
he glosses over the distinction between being the kind of failure
that indicates the need for a different social structure, "a humane order of society" and the kind which just hasn't had the
luck to be one of the privileged members of the one we have
("gifted with independent means"). It is a passage in which the
authorial ideology seems to be compensating for the disintegra-
tion of the fictional structure.

But both the placing of this passage and the relationship of
its "argument" to the novel as a whole make it much more than
this—help us, in fact, to understand the fictional function of
Reardon's story. In the first place, it comes after three chapters
which have not dealt with Reardon at all. The last time we have
seen Reardon, he has given up writing, rejected Amy's offer of

136

money, and begun to succumb to the London winter. The chapter
which this passage opens deals mainly with Biffen and his rescue
of the manuscript of *Mr. Bailey, Grocer* from the fire. At the
very end, Reardon is summoned to Brighton and in the following
chapter he dies. So that the passage comes after Reardon's role as
a literary producer is finished, long after he has become a decent
wage-earner. Secondly, the passage links Reardon and Biffen who,
except insofar as they are friends and live in poverty, have very
little in common. Biffen is a writer of real integrity who survives his poverty and is detached from the "weakly envious"
humour of Reardon. He will finally take his own life, but this
too is different from the squalid way in which Reardon lets himself die. It seems almost as though Gissing is trying to raise
Reardon on Biffen's bootstrings. Finally, we must bear in mind
the remarks about the kindly and imaginative virtues and independent means when we look at the end of the novel.

Reardon's story is about the end of a career. From the first
occasion on which we see him, he is merely struggling to defer an
end which seems inevitable. Whereas chapter three, the end of
the first episode, sees Milvain entering the fight, chapter six,
the end of the first episode of Reardon's story, defines him as a
finished man—"the spring of his volition seemed to be broken".
And whereas the second episode of the Marian story has at its
centre her negative epiphany in the British Museum, which constitutes the basis of her love for Milvain, the second episode of
the Reardon story shows him becoming more and more committed to mechanical work which is "work without hope". It is
as though we are meant to see the Marian story as having openings which are already closed in the Reardon story. The structure
continues this emphasis—Marian begins to look for a ray of
sunshine to penetrate the musty gloom of the museum at the end
of the episode which precedes the break-up of the Reardons'
marriage, and confronts her father during that episode which
portrays the final retreat of Reardon into poverty and loneliness.
In other words, the significance of Reardon in relation to the
story of Marian, and at the same time in relation to the minor
stories of Biffen and Whelpdale, is that of the already defeated
protagonist in the final act of a struggle to survive. His story
comments on the present as it continually recedes into the past

(the chapter headings "The Way Hither" and "The Past Revived" stress this). Every detail suggests this closure of possibilities. Travel, for example, is conventionally an opening in the realist novel, but for Reardon it is in the past, and its effect on the present is that it makes it more difficult to recover his early energies as a writer: "that vast broadening of my horizon lost me the command of my literary resources" (VI) (and he adds immediately that marriage too was an additional form of closure). Later, again talking to Milvain, he blames the badness of his most recent book on the three-decker system, but goes on to say that he could not make a living out of one-volume novels (XV). The action of the Reardon story is his return to the past, which is also a deliberate decision to end his literary career. More than that it is a retreat into a closed world. He becomes a "decent wage-earner" and moves to Islington. Amy moves back to Westbourne Park with her mother. Both resolve the social ambiguity of the literary life by abandoning it for a definite status and zone. This stress on the closing of possibility is a conscious rejection of the conventions of realist fiction. For it is as though Gissing has shifted an exemplary case to the centre to make the case of Reardon, which Milvain cites at the beginning as an example of how not to do it, the central dramatic interest of the novel. And that is because in his fiction typicality gives way to relativity: the protagonist does not sum up the possibilities of the world of the novel, but on the contrary registers its limits and determinants as a subjective crisis which comments on, without informing the energies still alive in that world. The explicit invitation to the reader's sympathy comes too late: it is less of an appeal than a sardonic recognition that the reader too is zoned in a world in which the individual case makes no difference. At the same time, for this very reason, it comes as an assault on the reader's sensibilities, poses the question of Reardon's failure against his own relative success.

But this is complicated by the link that is made between Reardon and Biffen. The episode which follows the address to the reader is the rescue of Biffen's manuscript from the fire, on which the dying Reardon later half humorously comments: "Don't say that authors can't be heroic" (XXXII). Biffen's "weakness" is of a wholly different order from Reardon's, for Biffen's "failure" can be confined to the level of his social deprivation. Starving in his garret, he "is not uncheerful" as he works "patiently, affectionately, scrupulously" on *Mr. Bailey, Grocer.* Moreover, whereas Reardon only writes fiction because he feels that it is the only way for the modern writer who can't journalise to make a living, Biffen embraces his own modernity with a modern aesthetic commitment. And although his poverty is much greater than Reardon's, he is without envy. Yet Biffen is no fool. In the discussions with Reardon, he shows a lot of commonsense which largely derives from the fact that, unlike Reardon, he is free of snobbery which makes Reardon so incapable of coping with necessity: "It is our duty to make the best of circumstances," he tells Reardon, "Why will you go cutting your loaf with a razor when you have a serviceable bread knife" (XXXI). Given his greater integrity and greater sanity, it is difficult not to feel that Biffen diminishes Reardon even further. And his suicide seems almost like a deliberate authorial strategy to keep us from seeing Biffen's approach to his career as a possible alternative value which can oppose Milvain.

However, the late emergence of Biffen as a more interesting protagonist than Reardon is part of a total strategy which controls the end of the novel. At the end of XIX, Reardon is no longer a man of letters —effectively his story is at an end. Yet this is only about half way through the novel. After this, except for the minor irony surrounding Amy's new fortune, Reardon's role becomes that largely of the wandering listener in literary London, visiting Biffen, calling on Whelpdale and going to see Sykes the drunken writer, who is a new character in the novel. At the same time, the novel begins to become increasingly episodic. Whelpdale suddenly tells of his struggles to make a living as a writer in America, Yule bumps into an ex-surgeon who tells of his misfortunes. This goes with an increasing self-consciousness on the part of the literary failures: Reardon dilating on Greek sunsets and humorously contemplating the absurd image of himself and Biffen, two "literary men", at a poor eating house, and Yule boasts that he is truly "a man of letters". Suddenly, from being a novel grimly concerned with the economics of authorship, *New Grub Street* is given over to an almost light-hearted record of the colourful squalor of literary life. The only major development in the action of the novel remaining is the rise of Milvain and his change of women. It is an odd effect: while Jasper is making it in society, the society of the novel becomes another world, a Grub Street in the eighteenth-century sense, with its own heroisms, comedies —almost a kind of comradeship. I say almost, because it is crucial that this only happens once Reardon's defeat is complete, and as Marian's way out begins to close up. Leslie Stephen describes Grub Street as "A region which, in later years, has ceased to be ashamed of itself, and has adopted the more pretentious name Bohemia" (*op. cit.*, p. 16). Bohemia is, of course, a mode of survival for artists in a society which cannot make them organic. It is the most obvious alternative to the Milvainic integration of literature with commerce as a whole. It constitutes itself as an autonomous social fraction in which aesthetic values can be protected against the market, at least to some extent. The story of Biffen together with the array of anecdotes and images which occupy so much of the last part of the novel, acknowledge this possibility. Yet, of course, it acknowledges it only to repress it. Despite a certain conviviality in these scenes, essentially it is on the fringe of a social grouping which cannot make itself autonomous. Biffen will die, ultimately, of loneliness. Whelpdale pushes himself into the commerce of literature in order to become a married man. Sykes remains a laughable eccentric.

The relative autonomy of the avant-garde, of Bohemia, is not ideologically available to Gissing, and I think we can understand this if, in conjunction with the word "practical", we consider another key term in the novel—independence. We have already seen how this concept acts as an ideological limitation in the authorial address when Gissing makes "independent means" an alternative to a mere humane society. Very briefly, Biffen ironises the term when Reardon expresses his habitual fear of the workhouse:

> I don't think I should be unhappy in the workhouse. I should have a certain satisfaction in the thought that I had forced society to support men. And then the absolute freedom from care! Why, its very much the same as being a man of independent fortune. (XXVII)

It reminds us of Milvain's comment on the man who has to be hanged—he too had forced society to specific measures. But both comments are jokes. Success and independence are too mutually supportive to allow this to become the basis of an alternative value. It is the point which the novel cannot go beyond, the question it deliberately doesn't ask. Independence has to remain the only possibility outside the market. At the same time, we recall that independence is a crucial concept in Besant's account of literary success, and that is precisely the note Milvain ends on. He is on the way to success because he has married Amy's money. "Oh you can afford to be more independent", she tells him, and a little later, when Jasper contemplates with satisfaction that he can now afford to be the generous man he wants to be and adds "Happiness is the root of virtue", she completes his thought with "And independence the root of happiness" (XXXVII). They are doing no more than learn the lesson of Reardon's failure. This constitutes the ideological limitation of the novel. The only solution to the problem of the disorganic literary class is for them to become part of the rentier class (or at least to have secure access to the profits of surplus value). But it also constitutes the specific effectivity of the novel. For Gissing has contrived a fiction which exposes not merely the Darwinian basis of the literary market, but also the reliance of that market on legalised expropriation. Literature is a trade, but a trade which cannot stand on its own feet. Which is the truth of all trades. The function of failure is not to oppose this "truth" but to reveal its way of working.

NOTES

1 Gissing, *New Grub Street*, edited with an introduction by Irving Howe (Boston, 1962).
2 Poole, pp. 105–35, and Chialant (1974) give valuable and complementary accounts of the context of *New Grub Street*. My purpose in this chapter is not to deny the importance of that "cultural" context which they define, but to account for the significance of the structure of the novel, which is different from its referential significance.
3 Stephen, *Samuel Johnson* (1895), p. 16. First published in 1887.
4 Besant – the following texts are referred to by date of publication: *All in a Garden Fair*, 3 vols. (1883); *The Pen and the Book* (1889); *Essays and Historiettes* (1903).

5

The Odd Women

1

At the end of the fourth chapter of *The Odd Women*, Rhoda Nunn, the novel's militant feminist protagonist, announces its theme to Monica Madden, who is to become her mirror, the oppressed wife. Pointing out that there are half a million more women than men she goes on:

> So many *odd* women—no making a pair with them. The pessimists call them useless, lost, futile lives. I, naturally—being one of them myself—take another view. I look upon them as a great reserve. When one woman vanishes in matrimony, the reserve offers a substitute for the world's work. True, they are not all trained yet—far from it. I want to help in that—to train the reserve. (IV)

It is a highly topical theme. Since the publication of Mills' *Subjection of Women* in the late 'sixties, there had been a developing feminist literature both challenging the place assigned to women within marriage and attending to the possibilities for a woman of a decent existence outside marriage. In the late 'eighties, Mona Caird had published an article recommending that marriage should be regarded as a business contract, and Harry Quilter had published a collection of letters called *Is Marriage a Failure?* Meredith had published a major novel, *Diana of the Crossways*, with a heroine who tries to make a living outside her marriage, James had published a scathing attack on American feminism which nevertheless presented a woman doctor, Mary Prance, with much admiration, and Hardy had already both in *The Woodlanders* and in *Tess of the D'Urbervilles* created two great novels which por-

142

trayed the specific oppression of woman by the economic, sexual and moral domination of a male culture. Unlike *New Grub Street*, *The Odd Women* has to be placed against other major achievements. We have to ask ourselves whether it can stand against such work as a distinctive achievement.

In order to do this, it is necessary to begin by defining Gissing's limitations. Neither of the two major ideological influences on Gissing, the rejected Comte or the partly endorsed Schopenhauer, would provide him with a motive for writing such a novel unless it was to show, like *The Bostonians*, the ultimate futility of "training" women. The first made woman, as wife and mother, the centre of a mystifying cult, and the second, inverting the cult, made her a child and an animal who at best was made to suffer the guilt of mankind through childbirth. Yet the oppression of woman is a constituent motif in Gissing's work from very early on. *A Life's Morning* and *The Emancipated* treat it explicitly, and in all the texts of the 'eighties woman is made to bear a very special role in the novels. Helen Norman is the register of the ideological ordeal of *Workers in the Dawn*, Ida Starr is the character who most squarely faces the moral contradictions of respectability in *The Unclassed*, Adela is the centre of the awareness of the inexorability of class division in *Demos*, and so on. In other words, in each of the novels the female protagonist is placed at the ideological frontier of the text's representativeness. This is partly because of the relative lack of mobility of women who are not therefore faced with a choice of action, so that while the male protagonist battles with circumstances, the female internalises the battle as an ideological drama. This has the effect of making them seem stronger and more decisive and at the same time more incapable of altering anything except by self-sacrifice. Ideologically, this is very anti-feminist, but only if we divorce it from the fictional structure. Gissing's fictional structure demands, as we have seen, a plotless network of circumstance in which the possibilities of liberation are confined to mental states. So that the actual effect seems like an idealisation: Helen, Ida, Thyrza, and so on, are privileged by their very oppression to understand the psychology of that oppression and thus escape the vacillations it imposes on those who are mobile. In other words, Gissing is precipitated towards the *Odd Women* by the demands of his own form.

On the face of it, this is to say nothing of Gissing which isn't true of many novelists. By its very nature, the novel tends to rely on woman as an epistemologically privileged register: its commitment to "realism", the representation of social interaction, implies two kinds of protagonist; the totalising consciousness which moves from one area of society to another—the footloose hero; and the fixed consciousness that from a place with a given "career" (courtship, marriage, motherhood) looks out on the social world as it offers itself as accommodation—initially the courted girl within the family. But there is a very specific development in the mid-nineteenth century which has to do with the break-down of convexity. As the footloose hero becomes the alienated intellectual, so the woman tends to become the wife: the fixed consciousness who has already undergone that career found it an oppression and has to make sense from within a trap. The very title of *Madame Bovary*, the heroine defined by a social accolade and a name not her own, is an index of this transition. Emma is not faced with a conflict between reality and romance. Her reality is "unreal" in the sense that her given world is a tissue of lies, hypocrisy, cliché and pomposity, and her own embraced and invented fictions, her romantic dreams, though they form a banality to escape a banality, are no more unreal than her daily world. But both offer prescribed roles—wife and adulteress. Nothing is ever *Emma* except the theatrical self-making of her suicide. Flaubert is, of course, an unsparing writer, and few novelists are so able to dispense with props from the ideology: nevertheless Emma is only a non-extreme version of the married woman portrayed in *Anna Karenina*, *Middlemarch*, *Portrait of A Lady* and, in a very different way, *Tess of the D'Urbervilles*. The shift from love to marriage as the central condition of the heroine's existence is one of the consequences of what Gissing terms himself "a more combative realism". In Emily Hood's mother, Adela Waltham and Miriam Bashe, he had incorporated this motif into his work.

Now let us look again at that theme stated by Rhoda Nunn. In the light of what has just been said: the ideological scrutiny of marriage in the 'eighties, and the fictional use of the marital trap, it begins to look very modest. Just as *New Grub Street* seems to limit itself to a narrow representation of the relations of literary production, unconcerned with the larger cultural implications, so *The Odd Women* seems here to involve itself with what is almost a side issue. For Rhoda Nunn is not talking about the oppression of women in general, but only about a surplus of women—the women who can't marry because there are not enough men to go round. They are a "reserve": "no making a pair with them" reinforces the oddity and seems to offer marriage as a norm. And this, to be sure, is one of the effects of the book. It is true that Monica marries and finds this a worse form of oppression than either her job as a shop assistant or the possible independence offered by Rhoda's school. But she only marries as an odd woman. That is, she doesn't marry by sexual selection; on the contrary, she marries a man she doesn't love in order to cope with what would otherwise be her superfluity. We shall see that the Monica-Widdowson relationship does interrogate marriage in a specific way, but, on the face of it, its failure does not challenge marriage as a norm. And although Everard Barfoot talks of mismarriage, his closest friend is one who marries very happily. Here then is a novel not about the oppression of women, but about the characteristics of spinsterhood, and its *raison d'etre* seems to be nothing deeper than a transitory statistic. What happens to its polemic when there are more men than women? It is true that the oddness is elaborated into a much larger theory both by Rhoda and by Mary Barfoot. Rhoda, for example, is prepared to despise "love" and advocate "a widespread revolt against the sexual instinct". But the actual novel really abandons the concept of oddness as an explicit object of attention—the whole plot as we shall see relies on the juxtaposition of "pairs", Rhoda and Barfoot, Monica and Widdowson—while the truly odd women, the elder Madden sisters, Miss Eade, the girl who takes to prostitution ("a not unimportant type of the odd women"), and Mildred Vesper, flit in and out of the plot as shadowy comments on the central drama. Oddness and the ideology springing from it comes to look provisional and specific.

There is a further limitation implicit in Rhoda's definition. Unmarried women only lead useless, lost lives if they are not working-class. Gissing has, from the very opening of the novel, stressed the genteel status of his protagonists. It is really because such women are brought up to be "ladies" that they are so hopeless outside marriage, and the Barfoot-Nunn establishment is explicitly concerned with a middle-class problem:

> Let those work for the lower classes (I must call them lower, for they are in every sense), let those work for them who have a call to do so. (V)

The great problem in feminism, of course, is the degree to which it should become a perspective for the total oppression of a social system. A pseudonymous writer of a letter reprinted in Quilter's book, *Glorified Spinster, Reading*, makes an explicit connection even when she is defending marriage: "women are an oppressed class and men are the oppressors". Marriage can either be seen as one form of systematic oppression (as Engels does) or as a specific anomaly. *Tess of the D'Urbervilles*, by having a working-class woman at its centre, precisely overcomes the narrowness of radical feminism in this way. But Gissing seems to repress that connection—though it is interesting that he feels the need to repress it explicitly. In short, Gissing is asking us to accept, as a novel clearly raising the question of the position of women, a fiction about a handful of middle-class women who have fallen foul of marriage. Ideologically it is very reactionary in its apparent radicalism. As we shall see, what motivates the feminism is a very oppressive social Darwinian ideology. For the present it is enough to remind ourselves that Rhoda agrees with Barfoot that recalcitrant wives should be beaten.

The novel does become a vehicle for the rehearsal of major questions about the position of women, and this is something that we shall return to. But unless we recognise fully these limitations, those ideas will seem to be cut adrift from the novel itself, for, like *Born in Exile*, much of the text constitutes a debate which is interesting in itself but which seems to be belied by the narrowness of the story. However, we can also say that these very limitations constitute a condition of its effectivity, for they arise from and motivate what is, for all its centrality of theme, a distinctly Gissing novel. The question of the oddness, for example, brings it within the bounds of the perspective from which all Gissing's major novels are written—that of the group of the unclassed.

146

That is, Gissing establishes oddness as a social characteristic, like exile, like writing, which yokes together different lives without constituting a community. At the same time, Gissing returns to what he had set up in *Demos*, the possibility of that community through the constitution of a self-conscious active group within the fictional group. Whereas socialism, however, was merely a contingent force, a threat to the dismembered consciousness, the Barfoot-Nunn school responds to it and tries to militate against its oppression. What they do is not despised, and it has the effect at least of raising the level of consciousness. By its exclusiveness, its insertion into a dominant social Darwinian ideology, however, it limits itself to the domain of the selected—ironically by "training" the odd women it makes oddness a more inexorable quality:

> Human weakness is a plea that has been much abused, and generally in an interested spirit. (XIII)

True this is Rhoda, and Mary Barfoot is more tolerant and understanding, but Rhoda has logic on her side and this logic is undermined by the actual experience of rejection—including her own. So that despite its political centre *The Odd Women* remains a novel about isolation and rejection. The pairings which dominate the plot are both failures—neither of them can overcome the isolating needs of their protagonists.

Secondly, the constitution of the theme as a middle-class problem is fictionally coherent with the other major constituent of the Gissing novel—its location in London. As in other works, London is an actuality, not a fictional world but a tissue of names and distances in which the made-up story passes unnoticed. And it is vitally important that two features of Gissing's metropolis are available to his characters. One is simply a limited mobility which exposes the characters to their own lack of location. More importantly in this novel, as earlier in *The Unclassed* and *Thyrza*, the novel encloses the pastoral world as holiday or excursion, so that characters are given the possibility of finite choice which is really no choice since holidays and excursions are conditional on reinsertion. And this is linked with a third feature, more developed in this novel than in any other that precedes it, and that is the concept of the suburb which is linked with marriage. Widdowson is distressed by Monica's mobility. When she reveals that she knows the quickest way home from Chelsea Bridge ("by train—from York Road to Walworth Road"), he seems to disapprove "this ready knowledge of London transit". "Transit" is overcome through marriage and its location is the suburb, Herne Hill, at once decentred and tied to the city, the enclosed pastoral of lower middle-class life. All these "possibilities" of relief from the city constitute a location which emphasises the oddness of the odd women. Exhausting walks, frustrating excursions, suburban dream prisons, these things make this novel very much a Gissing novel and enable him to view his "theme" from a special edge, the edge of the urban dispossessed whom nobody knows about. This in turn enables him to transform that theme into something very different from the rational account of it Rhoda gives. Oddness is special but its speciality is the rawness with which it confronts the material conditions of being a woman. Its larger perspectives are decentred.

2

Like *Born in Exile*, which is the story of a completed life, *The Odd Women* begins with a prelude removed in time and place from the main action. Here, the father of the Madden sisters, trying to maintain a genteel culture in a provincial town, sets up values which are to be mocked by the illusory nature of his own humanitarianism. "Let men grapple with the world", he says in Clevedon, but by his own inaction projects his daughters into the metropolitan struggle. "The home must be guarded against sordid cares", he goes on, but fails to see the frailty of the home's structure and the actual repression it relies on. He believes in a kind of progress too, which is to be mocked by the actual history of the novel: "human beings are not destined to struggle for ever like beasts of prey". Gissing is concerned with the portrayal of a present, but this present is given a past which is both cause of and contrast to the registered distress. This historicity and, what we have already noticed, the presence of a self-identifying active social group, make it seem that if we are not going to be offered the history of a single life, we are going to be presented with the history of a *social group*, unified by its history and by its self-consciousness. In other words, more than in any novel to date, Gissing seems to promise a totalised drama which will have a fictional and social meaning. The prelude launches the Madden sisters and Rhoda Nunn into the new world, and by the time we see them again, another form of totalisation has been set up—the co-ordination of layered individualities which constitute a social picture: the two eldest Madden sisters existing hopelessly in the only "career" (which is seen to be a form of enslavement) made possible by their disabling education, Monica caught between the shop-girl world of Walworth and the promise of suburban marriage, and Rhoda herself trying to organise new possibilities for the Odd Women. And this layering is given a plot by the interaction of a double chain—the contrasting stories of Monica and Widdowson and Rhoda and Everard Barfoot which are placed side by side until the last third of the novel when (after chapter 18) they begin to intersect. All these formal features promise us not, as in *New Grub Street*, or earlier in *The Nether World*, the *picture* of a social section, but a picture which is concatenated: a picture becoming a history.

And yet all these forms of totalisation turn out to be mockeries. Dr. Madden's ideas are understood only by the eldest Madden sisters who are quite incapable of learning to test them or live by them, and who don't, as it happens, play a major part in the story (so that there is an odd effect of the prelude launching them, which is confirmed by the opening chapter of the main action, and then the novel as a whole dropping them to concentrate on others, as though the past and its lessons must remain dumb). The opening of *Born in Exile* is a prelude to the history of the central character's life; this is the prelude to a background motif. Then the active group, though it is ideologically important, has little to do with the main action, since the group is committed to *odd women* whereas the main action concerns itself with the lives of couples. It is as though history and ideology motivated a background which comments separately on the foreground drama. This drama in itself is another undercut totality because the layers of experience never coalesce into a shared experience (there is no convex mirror—no-one can see the whole) and the action is, like the double action of *The Nether World*, a double chain which is never completed. *The Odd Women* is a novel whose very form constitutes a displacement of the representational possibilities of its "theme": it negates its own organic possibilities.

"No making a pair with them"—that is how Rhoda defines negatively the odd women—yet the main action revolves around two pairings: Monica and Widdowson, Rhoda and Barfoot. Does this mean that Gissing cannot cope formally with his subject, that he cannot bring himself to write a novel in which "love-problems" (George Eliot's term) aren't, as traditionally, the centre? At first it seems like it. The lonely odd women, Virginia and Alice Madden, for example, seem to be such passive victims that they can only be presented and then dropped. There is no possibility of making a story out of their misery, it is too static: Virginia has effectively only one "episode" which is when she walks from her lodgings in Lavender Hill to the Strand bookshops to buy a copy of *The Christian Year* for Monica's birthday—a two-hour walk which ends with her going into a public house for a brandy. This launches her on the road to alcoholism, while her sister takes refuge in another opiate, religion. Already their hopeless lives are plotted—they are really at an end as the main action begins. Equally, Monica's shop assistant colleague, Miss Eade, who takes to prostitution, has only two stages to her life—the frustration of her loneliness and the alienated fulfilment of her escape. Those characters who, on the other hand, try to make something of their oddness are so exceptional that they have to remain, in one way or another, background *ficelles*. Thus Mary Barfoot is, like her more militant and less practical rival Mrs. Cosgrove, present only as a commentator on the theme and the action, while her pupils are either, like Mildred Vesper, shadowy contrasts to the suffering protagonists or only present, like Bella Royston, as figures with a history acted out off-stage. The drama of the struggle is not fully worked out, the work of the campaigners is not portrayed. What appears to be the central conflict, the rivalry of Rhoda and Widdowson for the unformed life of Monica Madden, evaporates as soon as Monica is faced with a choice between a career and marriage, and Gissing seems to let go of it completely when he has Rhoda fall in love with Everard Barfoot and decide at the end of XIV that "love would no longer be the privilege of other women". She thus disqualifies herself as the leader of a group committed to what she has earlier called "a widespread revolt against sexual instinct" in order to rescue

women from the suffocating or alienating value called "love".
For all its practicality, the movement has a utopian irrelevance
because no one in the story can act out its demands on the individual life.

This limitation has to be acknowledged, but I think we should
try to accept the novel we actually have, and that means making
the negations of its organic possibilities the very bases of its positive effectiveness. And here we are to recall that the novel differen-
tiates itself from other novels of the period in not being explicitly
concerned with marriage. This seems to contradict the present
point which is that formally it operates not by dramatising its
explicit theme, oddness, but by dramatising pairings. The resolution of this is in the potential ambiguity of "no making a pair
with them". By it Rhoda simply means that for some women there
is no partner to be had. But it could also imply that even where
there is, pairing is impossible—made impossible by the whole
social condition of woman which confronts her with a choice
between the self-annihilation of marriage and the self-isolation of
spinsterhood. And indeed the two relationships which dominate
the action are precisely related to this condition. Monica's marriage is a negative action: it is a retreat from the fate of her
sisters, an attempt to overcome her oddness, having nothing to
do with any attraction to Widdowson. And the Rhoda-Barfoot
affair is the mirror image of this—the attempt on Rhoda's part
to carry the strength of oddness into the pairing situation. Gissing makes Monica and Rhoda centres of consciousness who carry
the isolate awareness of the odd women into the arena of sexual
politics, and he completes this structure by opposing their minds
to those of their male partners. So that the "pairs" of the novel
enact the exclusivity of their mutual points of view, and what we
might call the "spares" who people the novel's world underline
and extend that exclusivity. The odd women proper adumbrate a
world of norms which measure both the projection towards and
ultimate failure of the contrived pairings at the centre of the
drama. So to summarise the structure, the two relationships contrast with one another: within each the two protagonists oppose
one another not by open struggle but by the parallelism of their
lines of thought, and finally the ordinary world of marriage is
overturned because, by the use of background characters, oddness

is made to seem a normal condition. What all the characters, including the men, share with one another is their insuperable isolation, their oddness. Needless to say, it is a structure only made possible by its geography—London with its oppression of separated and contiguous streets, its treacherous possibilities of mobility, its enclosed arenas of pastoral escape.

After the opening two chapters of the main action (i.e. II and III) which consist very largely in description and dialogue setting up the Madden sisters against Rhoda Nunn, Gissing launches Monica as his first dramatised narrator in the third: what is instantly established is her mind aware of, but detached from, the world in which she finds herself—"the big ugly establishment" in which she works, the "usual conversation in the dormitory" among her colleagues which is "so little to her taste", and her hopelessly impecunious suitor. Equally she sees through the depressing triviality of her sisters. At the same time, significantly in reverie, she recalls in Church the first meeting, on an excursion to Richmond, with Widdowson. The parameters of Monica's destiny are thus realised as a disaffected consciousness and limited hopefulness—a hopefulness realisable in the enclosed escape of the Sunday trip, and ultimately in the enchained retreat of suburban marriage. Her elder sisters and Miss Eade constitute the co-ordinates of this consciousness, but so equally does the opportunity offered by Rhoda Nunn, an opportunity made concrete by the companionship of Mildred Vesper. But just as she is above the mediocrity of the victims, so she lacks Mildred's acquiescence in self-repression—"plain featured" and "studious", Mildred measures those unaccommodated sexual and social desires which "at nature's bidding" make it impossible that Monica should live alone. If the shop provides her with a specific oppression to rebel against, Monica's new work, which is liberated and human, demands a kind of heroism which merely depresses her. First out of the need to escape, and then out of the illness which declares the deeper frustration of the commitment to loneliness involved in being an effective odd woman, Monica is driven into marriage with a man for whom she feels no love.

Gissing traces Monica's marriage sharply and patiently. She is driven "at nature's bidding" from negation to negation. She marries to escape loneliness, and then Widdowson shows that his

Ruskinian chivalry can turn quickly to tyranny, jealousy, cupro-phobia and all the predictable characteristics of a man to whom marriage comes as a kind of pension after a lifelong servitude and loneliness. The chapter called "The Joys of Home" (XV) is an ironic rejoinder to "nature's bidding" which categorises Monica's decision to marry. From the start, Widdowson makes sure that joy is a matter of possessiveness ("Oh but I can't have you going about alone at night") and order (it is insisted on in detail after details, the obsession with punctuality, the adherence to routine and changelessness, the fear of other people). At first, Monica responds as an equal:

> "Now why can't we always live like this? What have we to do with other people? Let us be everything to each other, and forget that anyone else exists."
>
> "I can't help thinking that's a mistake." (XV)

The combination of sentimentality and repression in Widdowson is brilliantly done. Like Ruskin, whom he cites, he sets woman on a pedestal of chivalry only to keep her in her place, and it is a position that Monica can rationally oppose. But being married, she is caught, and resistance gives way to retreat ("Monica seemed to listen attentively, but before long she accustomed herself to wear this look whilst in truth she was thinking her own thoughts"), and retreat slides rapidly into strategy. She begins to develop an independent consciousness which she cannot share with her husband. And from this she is precipitated into another kind of romanticism, as banal as Widdowson's, that of the extra-marital flirtation with a man who cares about her less than her husband but who offers relief from the unnaturalness of her marriage and the promise of escape. In marriage as well as in single-ness, Monica remains isolated. Her "nature"—that is her sense of hope and youth—makes her travel, first to go to Richmond alone where she meets Widdowson, then to her lover's door. But she finds in Richmond only a parodic answer to nature's bidding —the answer of the "monument of male autocracy" (XV), and in Bayswater only the locked door of Bevis's apartment, the poor figure "trying to disguise his feebleness in tinsel phrases" (XXII). His final letter to her ironically sounds like an extract "from some vapid novel". Monica builds her image of escape on the novels she reads to console her for her life with Widdowson. Ultimately her revulsion from her husband is a rebellion against his viscosity: "His face was repulsive to her; the deep furrows, the red eyelids, the mottled skin moved her to loathing" (XXII). This is not trivial, it is the final response of a nature denied, but that nature finds expression in the most artificial kind of romance; it is not merely Bevis who is tinsel—his image retreats in her mind "like a lay figure" (XXVIII). It is *her own* vapid novel Monica is forced to write. London again. Widdowson has early objected to her "ready knowledge of London transit". London transit is the possibility of change, but not of a change responding to nature's bidding—only from the shop to the park, the villa to the apartment, spinsterhood, marriage, divorce, loneliness, viscosity, banality. Monica acts out the essential oddness of woman in a male autocracy.

What is remarkable is that Gissing seems to take over from Meredith a fictional structure which he then inverts. In Meredith, the male egoist is exposed, his artifices ironised by woman who brings to the web of images in which she is entangled, her "nature" which is also Nature. Monica moves from stage to stage at nature's bidding but it only leads her further into falsity and entrapment. This is partly because Gissing's egoist is not Willoughby Patterne but a pathetic middle-aged man whose rational grasp of life is as frail as that of his wife. Widdowson's mind is explored with as much detached compassion as Monica's: "Reason and tradition contended in him, to his ceaseless torment" (XIX). His tyranny comes from his essential isolation and his lack of strength. If his mind is totally made up about women ("he himself represented the guardian male, the wife proprietor who from the dawn of civilisation has taken abundant care that woman shall not outgrow her nonage"), he is nevertheless tormented by Monica's insistent individuality. He too is reduced to stealth, having to maintain his tyranny by using a detective, that is by exploiting the impersonality of London which makes it possible to set up what is explicitly, in a telling analogy, termed an "ambush" (XXIII). Gissing traces in as much detail as he does in the case of Monica the limited consciousness evolving towards a self-destructive assertion, for it is made clear that Widdowson by his very jealousy forces Monica to seek out another man. We could go on spelling out the details of this remarkably fine narrative, but the point is that both consciousnesses are evolved as separate and mutually exclusive points of view. The relationship is merely a trap which insists on their total separateness. Meredith's radical fictional structure relies on the possibility of "natural" relationships. In Gissing's novel this is impossible because the minds involved, both of them, are already too conditioned to have any real communication. Monica does not find herself in her marriage: she only confirms her loneliness. And Widdowson only finds the "other" in the turmoil of his isolation. The one point of contact is revulsion and fear. And this is placed as the psychology of bourgeois marriage—the detached suburban villa, apart from the world and yet shaped by it.

The Rhoda-Everard relationship is clearly at the opposite pole from this. Both characters are clearly more "modern" than Monica and Widdowson who both retreat into traditional roles. At the same time, instead of being an ordeal of reciprocal weakness, this is a trial of competing strengths. What both Rhoda and Everard have in common is a contempt for the traditional roles of marriage, and they respond to each other as a challenge. Rhoda especially sees Barfoot as a character in a "comedy". He takes her on as a matter of principle proposing a free union. She wishes to bring him to the point of proposing marriage. Both characters are self-conscious enough for Gissing to be explicit about it, and we don't need to spell out the evolution of this trial of strength. However, what does need to be analysed is the way in which the relationship relates to the odd women theme and the way it becomes entangled with the other story. In the earlier chapters, Rhoda presents herself as an anti-romantic social Darwinian. Marriage for her is merely an instance of the intrusion of human weakness, the personal life, into the social struggle, and the corruption of intelligence by the sentimentality of fiction. Barfoot is also sceptical about romantic illusion but his response is to see life as a spectacle, a "succession of modes of being", and this leads him to marked individualism ("The only thing that is clear to me is that I have a right to make the most of my life" [viii]). To some extent it is an ideological struggle between Comte and Schopenhauer. But equally it is a naked power game. This becomes evident once the two stories have acted on one another. It may seem factitious to have Rhoda led to believe that Barfoot is mixed up with Monica (though there is a strange affinity between these two which makes Barfoot open up to her and Widdowson jealous of him—perhaps a repressed mutuality), but Mary Barfoot's letter which creates the suspicion is only the catalyst which makes possible the confrontation of two unyielding and again mutually exclusive consciousnesses. Before the letter arrives, Barfoot is dissatisfied with their "affair" because he feels that he is losing, becoming more importunate than his opponent. What he is most conscious of is what he must "subdue", and he begins to see the prospect of marriage as "a long and bitter struggle for predominance". The arrival of the letter is a relief because he feels "almost glad of a ground of quarrel", and he deliberately sets out to provoke Rhoda's hostility. His rationalisation of his earlier affair with Amy Drake reveals him as unrepentant a sexist in his way as Widdowson, though earlier he has claimed that it is society that makes women like "criminals" (X). After the confrontation, he rejoices in his strength of will and awaits her submission which is the image of his erotic desire ("Oh but the submission would be perfect . . . then he would raise her").

Rhoda, on the other hand, is frustrated in a different way to begin with. She feels she has no "tact" and consoles herself with fanciful compromises:

> She was no longer one of the "odd women": fortune had—or seemed to have—been kind to her: none the less her sense of mission remained. No longer an example of perfect female independence, and unable therefore to use the same language as before, she might illustrate woman's claim of equality in marriage—if her experience proved no obstacle. (XXVI)

But, faced with the letter, and Barfoot's proud refusal to deny its truth, "she could not yield". Her notional acceptance of Barfoot is lowering herself enough and in this further challenge she must "prevail": "the incredulity she could not help must either part them for ever, or be to her an occasion of *new triumph*" (my italics). In real terms, the ground of the quarrel is trivial: Rhoda soon finds out that Barfoot is innocent. But it does hold them apart, for she waits for him to come to her, and he doesn't. For him, the retreat into the most conventional of marriages. For her, the return to her work, ironically with Barfoot's Schopenhauerian pride:

> Passion had a new significance: her conception of life was larger, more liberal: she made no vows to crush the natural instincts. But her conscience, her sincerity should not suffer. (XXVII).

"Preserve one's soul alive"—that phrase, which in 1886, when Gissing wrote it, was effectively an endorsement of a kind of tory dandyism, has a new significance in this novel. It implies not escape but survival, and that is what the novel is about— what it takes to survive as a woman. Rhoda at the end is at her most odd. No longer simply at one with the cause, but neither given over to love: the isolate soul, the ego that cannot be inserted into the group. And yet, at the very end, we see her playing with the dead Monica's child, bringing news of the flourishing cause and feeling sadness at the tragedy represented by the baby. Preserving one's soul alive is not an option—it is a necessity in a world in which all the forms of belonging insist on one's oddity and refuse to hear one's natural voice.

3

On the face of it, *The Odd Women* is a doubly frustrating novel. Announcing itself as a text about the situation of women, the theme, as we have seen, is rapidly specialised—it is only to be about displaced middle-class women and their struggle to survive. We can accept this on the grounds that, as in Gissing's work as a whole, this kind of specificity is experimental: the atypical displacement of his characters constitutes a laboratory in which the odd protagonists confront at the point of maximum oppression the negations of the incorporated social world. But a second level of frustration enters in at this point. The narrative realisation of this confrontation is further displaced from the theme: the oddness is not dramatised as oddness at all but as a double narrative of personal relationships. Oddness, the predicament of the unselected, is only present as an abyss— a warning or a norm which precipitates pairings. It is tempting to Hegelianise our reading and see this formal contradiction of the ideological

specificity as the negation of a negation, as though Gissing re-
centres his narrative by making his protagonists face a more
"typical" situation, that of love and marriage. To do so, however,
would not only be to explain the novel away as a pointless circu-
larity, but would also ignore the actual quality of the relationships
which have been presented: the Monica-Widdowson relationship,
although it incorporates a central dominant ideology of marriage
(Widdowson's attempt to impose Ruskin's appropriation of romantic infatuation for a repressive order), isn't a real test of marriage
since it is from the start merely an escape from oppressive isolation which holds no real promise. To put it simply, we are never
invited to think of Monica's marriage as an index of marriage in
general. Ruskin certainly wouldn't approve of it. And this lack of
typicality seems to be stressed by the fact that the example of
happy marriage in the novel, that of Micklethwaite, is equally
Ruskinian. Everard tells him:

> My own views are rather extreme, perhaps; strictly I don't be-
> lieve in marriage at all. And I haven't anything like the respect
> for women, as women, that you have. You belong to the Ruskin
> school. (IX)

He characterises Micklethwaite as "old fashioned" but his own
views are in the end disabling. For if Monica's Ruskinian trap is
the product of her threatening "oddness" and thus preordained,
so Barfoot's involvement with Rhoda is a Darwinian battle that
derives from their mutually incompatible versions of modernity,
precisely because what characterises that modernity is a rational
egoism. Neither relationship then challenges the possibility of
marriage as such. The "odd" women who people the sidestreets
of these doomed non-relationships do not form any kind of contrast. Rather it is that Monica and Rhoda dramatise a specific
development of that exclusion. The fictional form does not undermine the ideological specificity, it redoubles it—a special aspect
of a special group, the displacement of the displaced. The pastoral
locations of the affairs, Richmond/Herne Hill and the Lake District, are only specific forms of the urbanisation which is the odd
woman's only incorporation.

At the same time, in terms of explicit discussion, the novel,
as I said at the beginning, is topical and its topicality includes a

very wide-ranging discussion of the major issues of sexual politics. It even includes a lecture on the future of "Woman as Invader". Does this mean we are faced with what many have seen as a typical Gissing case in which an intellectual enquiry sits undigested in a story of marginal significance—is Gissing's ability as a writer unable to measure up to his involvement with progressive ideas?

Mary Barfoot's lecture (XIV) is the obvious focus for a resolution of this problem. She begins with a specific issue, the question of "her encouragement of female competition in the clerkly world" which increases hardship by the underselling of labour. She justifies this on the grounds that "in the miserable disorder of our social state" one has to decide to alleviate one grievance at the expense of another, and the more pressing grievance for her is the exclusion of women from a sphere which would extend the possibilities of their becoming "rational and responsible human beings". The so-called womanly professions of hospital nurse and governess inhibit this development because they keep women in their "proper sphere" (i.e. they are versions of motherhood), whereas Mary wishes them to become "conscious of their souls" and to be startled into "healthy activity". This is linked with what is seen to be a "revolutionary" commitment: "I am a troublesome, aggressive, revolutionary person." It is the only positive response to the actual historical situation which is "a time of warfare, of revolt". And it is equally an educational revolt, an invasion which will both demand and create "a new type of woman, active in every sphere of life". The specific issue of jobs is thus transposed onto a more general level—it is part of the tactics of changing the image of "the nature of woman". In other words, the practical concern is part of an ideological struggle.

"What we call the nature of women is an eminently artificial thing": with this sentence John Stuart Mill makes it necessary to see the subjection of women not as a legal arrangement which can be overturned by technical emancipation, but as a deeply rooted cultural oppression which attempts to derive a "natural" temperament for woman from her customary role as wife and mother. (It took Engels, however, to analyse that customary role as the result of the social relation of production in capitalist society.)

Mary Barfoot is precisely responsive to this level: the issue of what jobs women should take entails the question of what constitutes the "womanliness" of woman. "Womanly" is an ideological term of much power in the late nineteenth-century reaction to feminism—Mrs. Lynn Linton opposed the "womanly woman" to the "shrieking sisterhood"—and Mary Barfoot tries to rescue it from what she sees it as truly denoting, which she defines as womanishness.[1] Insofar as women are "womanly" in the false sense, their natural growth is stunted. The theme is picked up later by Everard Barfoot who by and large despises women, but acknowledges too that they are like the criminal class—creatures of a society which blames them for being what it has made them. Again, Widdowson defensively thinks of women as "simply incapable of attaining maturity" (XIX). And to some extent this is acted out in the novel by the Madden sisters who are essentially no more than girls deprived of a father (Monica marries Widdowson because she respects him and he gives her security: Alice and Virginia are always hoping to become "new women" but as Mary says of the Madden sisters "They all strike me as so childish" [VI]).

Thus the novel engages with sexual politics at least at the level of ideology (as opposed merely to that of what Gramsci terms "state coercive power"), and further than this, though marginally, by the account of the oppression of women in terms of working conditions, at the level of the social relations of production. Is this, however, merely a "lecture"? I think not. Mary's polemic is given a specific dramatic context: she has been involved in an emotive disagreement with Rhoda about one of the trainees who has eloped. Rhoda's theoretical rigour has no mercy and Mary has to remind her that "to work for women one must keep one's womanhood" (XIII). Mary's lecture is an assertion of theoretical militancy in the face of her pragmatic moderation over the specific case. The school as a whole too has to define itself against the more "revolutionary" ideology of Mrs. Cosgrove (which turns out to be a politicised version of bohemian élitism). In other words, the ideological analysis arises from a constricting actuality, a state of warfare it is true, but one in which the enemy is not merely the social structure but the very "nature" (that is socially necessary temperament) of woman. The enemy is the invisible force which projects women along the line of their destiny, keeping their knowledge of transit within the city, within the codes prescribed by their education, their aspiration and the places allowed them.

The odd woman is forced to seek her womanliness within the trap which the selectivity of a "free" society lays for her. Because it is a doomed search—a search which ends in defeat or stalemate which only offers the suburb at the end of the path, or public house at the end of the walk—it is a search which reveals in an extreme way the confusion of womanliness and womanishness. The odd woman, alone or in the more violent isolation of sexual relations, measures the "nature" of woman at the point where it is no longer sustained by the artifices of incorporation. The ideological specificity and its redoubled specialisation in the fictional realisation brings the odd woman up against the terms which are offered by the task of survival. In war the casualties are the most graphic reminder of the need for victory and the most challenging sign of the intransigence of what is fought against. The odd woman is the index of the violence of the existing order. Speaking to us from the silence left by the voice of power, she is the object of a question—what are we to do with those we cannot fit in? But equally she asks, as she elicits that specific question, a question of that question. What kind of world is it that depends on exclusions? It is the question of Gissing's urban vision: what kind of "nature" does the city force from us? The novel is the most truly experimental Gissing wrote. For it demonstrates, as the function of its limitations of theme and realisation, the very laws that encompass the world beyond it. In that passage with which I began, Rhoda, ideologically accepting the notion of a reserve, nevertheless tacitly comments on the world her campaign lies outside: "when one woman *vanishes* into matrimony," she says, "the reserve offers a substitute for the world's work." The odd women will not vanish—they are incapable or unwilling to accept the proffered annihilation. The armies of the night, ignorant and wounded though they are, besiege the citizens of broad daylight. The reserve, the residuum, measures the terms of incorporation.

NOTE

1 I have dealt with the literary manifestation of this concept in "Woman
and the Literary Text", in Mitchell and Oakley (eds.), *The Rights and
Wrongs of Women* (1976), pp. 217–55.

6

In the Year of the Jubilee

1

I have located a specific fictional space in which Gissing's novels exist, a space determined by a fictional terrain which is presented in a specific way and a protagonist who moves around in that terrain carrying the burden of a specific contradiction—that feeling himself ultimately alone (unclassed, exiled, locked in Darwinian combat) is nevertheless determined by his belonging to a group which holds and motivates him. The grouping intensifies the isolation because it creates competition. In addition, the location of the protagonists' struggles for survival has a double function of zoning and transit, thus offering mobility without freedom and entrapment without shelter. This provides a larger engroupment which situates the immediate issue of the novel (production of books, liberation of women) in an apparent "void" which is the geography of capitalist production. The generative distributive city is rarely "imaged" as it is in Dickens, or later, in Dreiser, because it is Gissing's specific contribution to the novel of urbanisation to motivate his fictions as isolated segments of the total process. But the total process is always there, a brooding absence which drives these atoms into their obscurity.

In the Year of the Jubilee looks, in these terms, to be a new departure for Gissing, and to some extent it is. The social-economic grouping here is much looser, and we are not faced with a city which only tolerates those who pass through its thoroughfare or keeps those whose labour it needs in their place. On the contrary, we are in the highly desirable suburb of Camberwell, and we are involved in the lives of characters who are not totally conditioned by the struggle to survive, partly because they have

163

parents who have made it unnecessary. The very opening has a very unGissing-like note:

> De Crespigny Park, a thoroughfare connecting Grove Lane, Camberwell, with Denmark Hill, presents a double row of similar dwellings: its clean breadth, with foliage of trees and shrubs in front gardens, makes it pleasant to the eye that finds pleasure in suburban London.

The exact naming of the streets is part of Gissing's regular fictional technique but the irony is very different: for once it is a genuinely ambiguous irony—it is almost possible to take pleasure in the image offered; "clean", "breadth", and the sense of greenery actually entice the reader before he is dropped into the humiliation of that last phrase. By the time the next sentence has arrived we're involved with middle-class complacence, respectability and buff brick—but for a moment we are free to enjoy the suburban breadth.

Why? Because in *In the Year of the Jubilee* Gissing concerns himself for the first time with what it's all *for*. For a decade and a half he has been writing novels about those who service capitalism, or get pushed aside by it, or who try to oppose it rashly. But Camberwell is not, like Clerkenwell or Lambeth, a productive zone. Nor is it that indifferent central area in which Reardon or the Madden sisters find themselves. On the contrary, it is the world of the desirable residence. And this seems to be stressed further by the title. Gissing often dates his novels with some precision. But here he impregnates the dating with a general symbolic significance. Jubilees are celebrations, and since they are generally bound up with the passage of time, the celebration entails a review: where have we come to. So the Jubilee itself poses the question of "progress". The suburb and the Jubilee—the space and time of "the ambitious middle class". Until now Gissing's fiction has dealt almost exclusively with the meaning of failure: this is a novel whose starting-point is success.

Suburbs are complex affairs.[1] Obviously they are a response to pressure on space—as the city changes from a distributive or passive function to an industrial or generative function it has to create a larger and larger working class which crowds and devalues the inner centre. There is thus a middle-class demand for housing

which can be satisfied as transport makes urban transit "normal",
and as land from the great landed estates becomes available so
that the speculative builder can reproduce on a large scale the
individual houses that the middle class think they need. Equally
this middle class must grow because in order for capitalism, which
is essentially the production of exchange value, to go on increasing its output of surplus value, it has to create markets over and
above the market for needs. Thus it is essential that although the
surplus value created by production is appropriated by a relatively
small and continually decreasing number of capitalists, it should
be continually redistributed in the form of ground rents, interest
and payment for services, so that the middle class proper—i.e.
the capitalist class—needs not only its workers, but also a
whole army of dependents, clerks, professionals, even investors
and landlords, who help him cope with the developing scale of
production but, more importantly, constitute a market for expansion. The suburbanisation process, as David Harvey has
pointed out, is a central feature of the expansion of production.
Suburbs thus are at once reflections of the productive development of the city and generative forces within the city. One of the
most notable features of the novel is that the money which
finances the protagonists all comes from sources whose market
is the suburb itself. The French money is from building: the Lord
money from piano-making, Peachey sells disinfectants; and Tarrant lives off money made from the manufacture of black lead.
Equally Beatrice French and Luckworth Crewe service this market
through fashion and the provision of holidays. Camberwell is
both a function of the urban centre and a self-perpetuating en-
tity in a redistributive complex which keeps the surplus in circulation.

The opening section of the novel registers this space very
precisely. The first page initiates the essential features of its
structure which are elaborated through the novel but which above
all make possible a plot which exposes the meaning of suburbanisation itself. In that sentence I have quoted, the word "suburban"
alerts us to the specific categorisation of the locality which is
further intensified by the naming of Camberwell. Camberwell, as
readers of Matthew Arnold would have known, indicates the land

of the philistine, and indeed the most settled, representative character, Samuel Barmby, is later described as a suburban deity. Tarrant describes Nancy Lord's qualms at being found with him in his rooms as "Camberwellism". He also calls it "provincialism", and in many respects that is what Camberwell indicates—a provincial enclave within the metropolis. And yet it is more than that: if it is defined by its lack of sophistication, it is also determined by its proximity to the centre, for it is not an independent world even though it is, in some ways, autonomous. The paradox of the suburb is partly expressed in the "clean breadth" of the "thoroughfare". The suburb is essentially a network of enclosed spaces, pastoral voids which function as retreats and expressions of urban capitalism. The Lords' garden is described with representative accuracy:

> The garden was but a strip of ground, bounded by walls of four feet high: in the midst stood a laburnum, now heavy with golden bloom, and at the end grew a holly bush, flanked with laurels . . . Nancy seated herself on a rustic bench.
>
> (I, iv)

A walled-in rusticity indicates a precisely bounded pastoral, and this is born out by many other details of the novel and on many different levels. At the beginning, Arthur Peachey is going away on holiday, and holidays are to be a central feature of the novel—it is at Teignmouth that Nancy is seduced by Lionel Tarrant, and at Bournemouth where her brother gets entangled with Fanny French. The commercialisation of Whitsand is Luckworth Crewe's way of exploiting the suburban market. The suburb encloses space for the enjoyment of those who produce and demand the wealth which generates an urban society. It is away from the city but its very existence depends on rapid transit. One of the recurrent images in the novel is public transport—in the first section there is a tram-ride to the centre to see the Jubilee celebrations. Later, when Nancy is on her own in South London, her consciousness focusses on a tram-conductor's shouts. The suburb makes for stasis: "Each house seems to remind its neighbour, with all the complacence expressible in buff brick, that in this locality lodgings are *not* to let." It is a world to put down

166

roots in, but at the same time there has to be rapid mobility both to supply the wealth and to escape its limitations.

On another level, the aspirations of the locality confirm this duality. The name of the Peachey road is "De Crespigny Park" and although what this primarily reflects is the breaking up of great landed estates into building plots, the very persistence of the names, "park", "estate", and so on, recalls the parodic nature of the suburb. For what are country estates except precisely larger versions of the walled garden? Dyos stresses that suburban housing serves an extreme individualism (the Englishman's home is his castle) *and* a persistent imitativeness. The Peachey house is unattached, but it is one of a double row of identical buildings. The stucco pillars echo the manor that it has displaced. At a lower social level, in the Morgans' household, the parodic nature of suburban development is expressed more explicitly: the manor is broken up, the new estate dignified with the name of Park, and the spacious houses begin to crumble with damp as the manor house itself is broken up. This imitation/individuation paradox is evident at very different levels. Nancy Lord's conception of culture, for example, is the emulation of good taste. Samuel Barmby's conception of knowledge is information from the paper, and the most obvious cultural victim of the suburban process, Jessica Morgan, is trying to train herself to pass examinations. If, on the one hand, Luckworth Crewe is able to make money by the exploitation of holidays, on the other Beatrice French operates through the need of women to imitate their metropolitan superiors through fashion.

All that I have said so far is that the novel "reflects" suburbanism both in its physical environment and in the specific location of middle-class desires in the paradoxes of urban culture. But it is much more dynamic than this. The striking images of the first part of the novel are those of Arthur Peachey quietly escaping from his own home, and Nancy Lord looking out of her front room window, "a hand grasping each side of her waist", poised on the edge of boredom. Two kinds of psychological tension emerge as the specific tensions of suburban life: a generational tension and a marital tension. Stephen Lord is a self-made businessman, but he can only create a vacancy for his children. There is no reason for them to work and they emerge only as frustrated consumers. The son, Horace, is merely a weakling who is the willing victim of Fanny French's wiles and the lucky receiver of his mother's superior schemes. But Nancy is at the centre of the novel and it is on her that Gissing visits the tensions of suburban life. The suburb is a dormitory for the man who makes enough money to live there. But for his wife and daughters it is a whole world. There is nothing for them to do but inhabit the space that has been purchased. Nancy is frustrated by her father's refusal to move into a better house, frustrated by her lack of culture, frustrated ultimately by her womanhood which means, in this context, by her unnecessary existence. Poised between escape routes— Luckworth Crewe and Lionel Tarrant—she is trapped even after Stephen Lord's death in the suburban stasis. But Nancy's thwarted energies are reflected in a different way by all the women in this novel: even Ada Peachey is a trapped suburban housewife and we cannot help sensing in the outbursts of rage and petulance a refusal to accept the deadly role she is offered (a role which reproduces that of Monica Widdowson). Marriage and the family are the sacred tasks of the suburb, giving safety, space and stability within the urban turmoil. And marriage and the family are precisely what are breaking up, precisely what are called into question by the very paradoxes of suburban living. So that although we are faced with a very different novel from any that Gissing has written before, that difference cannot be expressed simply as a development from a concern with failure to a concern with success. For if suburban life is a product of success and a guarantee of survival, it is also self-defeating. What it seeks to escape, it harbours, and what it attempts to generate, it undermines. The soirée at the Peacheys' sums it up: it is an "at home" by which the homecoming owner is made homeless, an evening of "culture" which is mindless. Within the suburban spaces, the animal energy it houses dooms its very success to failure. The disturbed household, the broken marriage, the reckless children are generated by the same energies which built homes to escape them. Stephen Lord, faced with his son's infatuation with a trollop, says that soon there will be no such thing as home: but his home was built on his own marriage with a trollop. *In the Year of the Jubilee* is still about failure, but it is the failure not of society's victims, rather of its own aspirations.

2

What we have in the opening sections of the novel is the creation of a total world of the suburb—the middle-class dream which is also the focus of middle-class frustration, the oppressive contingencies of vicarious leisure. Much of the story follows through the frustrated energies of the women imprisoned in this dream. Nancy herself is caught between two sources of energy outside the suburb—the commercial romanticism of Luckworth Crewe and the cultured scepticism of Lionel Tarrant. Both are forms of escape for her, though they are also, as we shall see, products of the same ethos that produces the urban trap. The point is that she is left staring out of the front room window, and that only by joining the crowd for the Jubilee or taking a holiday can she find a way of expressing what she has inside her. This sense that the suburban world encloses without endorsing the individuality which it appears to celebrate is reflected in different ways in the distorted energies of the French sisters or Jessica, and Gissing very sharply realises this continual fiction—Nancy's flight to the jubilee, Fanny French's frustration, Beatrice's cynicism; it is like a jungle trapped in the walled garden. In many detailed ways, a pervasive nervous energy transmits itself: boredom, imitation and bitchiness characterise the general tone of the conversations. Put this way, it may seem that the novel adds up to no more than a cliché—the penalties of affluence. Partly this is belied by the simple accumulation of detail and by the way in which facile social judgments (which are certainly imported into the style by overt authorial commentary) are contested by the unity imposed on this detail by the suburban focus. So that, however Ada Peachey, for example, is categorised as a totally animal wife who can do nothing but fight with her servants, or her sister Fanny as a tart with candy floss respectability, the fact that they are in the same context as Nancy Lord, with the same limited perspectives and repressed energies—the fact, in short, that they are part of the suburban world, that this is a world built up carefully by the observation of objects and the revelation of tensions—makes the distance not one of Arnoldian disdain but rather that of the experimental novelist making a structure which will carry the weight of these tensions.

The question is whether Gissing manages to generate a story which does justice to the social image conjured up in the first section. On the face of it, the answer seems to be no. By the end of the second section Nancy is committed to Tarrant who is above "Camberwellism", and the rest of the novel seems to be about her coming to terms with his egoism and his minor modification of his scepticism about marriage. The suburban theme seems to retreat into the background to erupt only occasionally, admittedly in some very fine scenes: most notably Arthur Peachey's confrontation with the failure of his marriage, and to a lesser, more schematic extent, with Jessica Morgan's breakdown and effective intellectual suicide. At its worst, the novel gets entangled in a melodramatic plot centering on Nancy's brother, her disguised mother and the fallen Fanny French with whom he is infatuated. The problem is bound up with the title. The Jubilee itself seems, as I have said, to provide a "time" for the suburban space. A history of progress, it also offers the possibility of a historicity. But this too disappears. Luckworth Crewe, the spirit of the jubilee, remains very much a background figure.

I think that to some extent this has to be admitted: *In the Year of the Jubilee* hovers uneasily between panorama and ideological fable. It is as though the tensions latent in the whole complex of stories initiated at the beginning become split into levels—expositional (Nancy and Tarrant and the commentary on hugger-mugger marriage), exemplary (Arthur Peachey and the way to deal with bad wives), and sensational (the intrigue of Nancy's returning mother which seems to rely heavily on *East Lynne*). But if this is true, it is also true that the progression of the story focusses the panoramic structure on sexual politics which is quite unlike anything earlier in Gissing, and if he retreats into his own churlish ideology at the end, it is only because he confronts issues which are not, in his terms, soluble. And to see that, we have to take account of the Jubilee and Nancy's absent lover, Luckworth Crewe.

The suburb gives expression and permanence to prosperity, but it is made possible by mobility. It is essentially a place where middle-class women are kept, but also, because the man is still

170

committed to another place, the place of business, where they are left alone to work out their own responses to their frustrations. Nancy Lord has two ways out of her mediocrity, and both are present as she stares out of her front window: on the table is a book about evolution, outside not visible but present in her conscious mind is the "gathering tumult of popular enthusiasm". The book and her student friend are admission tickets to the Tarrant family with its easier accommodation of wealth and the intellectual sophistication of the present heir. The gathering tumult is part of the energy which she is heiress to and yet denied expression for—the great commercial leap forward of Victorian Britain which the Jubilee celebrated. Her dowdy home and her limited status as a woman cut her off from both of these possible modes of expression. She cannot really educate herself—and she hasn't really any call to a profession. But the suburb has its contingent openings. Arthur Peachey is off on holiday. Holidays are specific forms of pastoral; you go to *resorts* to have holidays — it is a very urban concept, the holiday, requiring a far flung suburb which takes to an extreme the enclosed spaces of the urban park. On holiday, in Teignmouth, Nancy will be seduced by Lionel Tarrant. But first there is another rejected possibility, and this comes from the other mode of pastoral offered to the suburb, and that is the excursion.

Excursion to the centre, to the original centre which generates the suburb and from which it flees. The suburb comes into being as a result of rapid transit: "At Camberwell Green they mingled with a confused rush of hilarious crowds, amid a clattering of cabs and omnibuses, a jingling of tram-car bells" (I, vii). Nancy goes to the Jubilee celebrations, not to commit herself to its meaning (she disdains that, and doesn't go to the actual procession) but to see the illuminations and to mingle with the crowd. It is an unfocussed escape and one which is strictly limited—she can only go on condition that she accepts the protectorship of the suburban deity Samuel Barmby. We would expect Gissing to write about the Jubilee as he had written about the daytrip to Crystal Palace in *The Nether World*, that is with a classicist's detached ironic sense of the degeneracy of communal rituals in modern society. To some extent he does, but he has set the Jubilee up for Nancy who is seeking life, and compared with the stagnant uncertainties of Grove Lane, what essentially emerges is its vitality. The tumult is a form of integration: the class distances which the suburb monumentalises are broken down. When a fight breaks out, she laughs. She schemes for her brother to get free to meet Fanny and feels increasingly the oppression of Barmby's protection. It is a momentary liberation: the tram-car takes her back to the turmoil of her origins, the basic but good-humoured struggle for survival amid the crowds, amidst whom she meets, like a genius of the celebrations with "coarse but strong features vivid with festive energy", Luckworth Crewe.

Crewe has all the vigour of Milvain with none of Milvain's calculating meanness. What he offers Nancy is a kind of pastoral release from her own uncertainties. On their assignation he takes her up the Monument which celebrates the destruction of the old city and its rebuilding in the early stages of modern capitalism. The streets of London for Crewe are "so many chapters of romance, but a romance always of today, for he neither knew nor cared about historic associations" (II, iii), and his total commitment to the present is evident in the basis of his commercial enterprise—advertising:

> Till advertising sprang up, the world was barbarous. Do you suppose people kept themselves clean before they were reminded at every corner of the benefits of soap? Do you suppose they were healthy before every wall and hoarding told them what medicine to take for their ailments?
>
> (I, viii)

Significantly, Crewe is reporting the sale of advertising space to an obstinate client. He is advertising advertising, and the impression he makes on Nancy is one of "knowledge, acuteness, power". Gissing is undoubtedly ironising Crewe, but Crewe remains the one character in the novel with a certain identity and an inviolable integrity. He really does try to give Nancy a future, and he really does help Beatrice French in her business enterprise. When Nancy feels that he enables her to live in the present and that this is worth more than "oceans of culture", we can see what she means: in contrast Tarrant seems like a prig and Barmby like a stupid boor (Barmby is a suburban deity, but, with his half-baked philistine culture, he is a mere reflex of the creative energies of the City).

But the Monument, the place Crewe takes her to, has another significance. The Monument is essentially an image of success. You climb the stairs to an observation platform from which you can look down on the world:

> As soon as she had recovered from the first impression, this spectacle of a world's wonder served only to exhilarate her; she was not awed by what she looked upon. In her conceit of self-importance she stood there, above the battling millions of men, proof against mystery and dread, untouched by the voices of the past, and in the present seeing only common things, though from an odd point of view. Here her senses seemed to make literal the assumption by which her mind had always been directed: that she—Nancy Lord—was the mid point of the universe.
>
> (II, iii)

It is a passage which is crucial for the novel as whole in a way that is rare in Gissing, and it says much about his technique that its significance is one that the outcome of events *negates*. Above all, of course, Nancy is to go through an experience which precisely displaces the assumption made literal by the "odd point of view". She is to be, immediately after this, "nature's graduate" by submitting to the conjuncture of Tarrant's personality and her own sexual and social aspirations. And she is to end, married and subjected, by making "a virtue of necessity", determined by her past, made compliant by the mystery and dread of the alternative aloneness. At the low point of her fortunes, she walks about South London, listening to a bus-conductor shouting "London Bridge" which reminds her of this day, the moment when she seems to be put on top of the struggle for survival.

So the Monument offers a literal correlative of the egoism which drives her into the necessity of self-abnegation. It is a delusion, but a delusion which clarifies the contradictions of her life. In the first place, the conceit of self-importance which puts her above the "battling millions of men" is only reached by a long climb to the top—that is by climbing out of the multitude through struggle. She and Crewe exchange a series of loaded jokes about climbing and falling which makes this significance clear. Put another way, the Monument platform is above the City but it is also of the City. The conceit is partly so because it momentarily rewards the struggling ego with the idea that he is above the struggle. Secondly, and more importantly, Nancy has been taken there by Crewe, who has precisely sold himself to Nancy on the grounds of his own superiority: "There are not many men down yonder . . . who have a better head for making money." Ironically, this city genius, the self-made man from the north, has an image of success which is what lies behind the suburban ideal—a country house, a model farm and pictures. The particular line of business is important here. For Crewe is not like those self-made men of the mid-Victorian novel: he does not produce goods, does not even work in their sense. Rather he sells, and what he sells are images—advertising—the modern science which makes suburbia what it is—clean, healthy, endlessly aspiring to greater consumer power. Crewe is fundamentally a man of the Jubilee which in itself was a great feat of publicity and image-making happening after Britain had already begun to lose its predominance in the area of production and technology. The battle of the millions which they look down on is a battle for markets won by images—and what they have is images; "seeing only common things but from an odd point of view" might exactly describe the aim of advertising.

On the one hand, therefore, a father who produces for the suburban market relying on credit, on the other, a lover who promises a fortune from the agitation of the markets of the generative city: Nancy's moment of atavistic recovery of the primal energies of the city is ironically an engagement with the ultimate agent of the circulation process. What is crucial is that she is a woman, for woman is the focus of suburban contradictions. And Crewe, with his capacity to create images for the ego, has a very suburban view of women. Here, in this passage, he mentions that one of his great desires is to "see my wife's portrait in the Academy". She must be beautiful and he must be rich enough to pay the artist. His proposition is that she will wait for him to make his money—give him two years "to show that something worth talking about is to come". But the other side of this heroic commercial chivalry is his comment earlier to Beatrice French:

> Let women be as independent as they like as long as they're not married. I never think the worse of them, whatever they do

that's honest. But a wife must play second fiddle, and think her husband a small god almighty—that's my way of looking at the question.

(II, ii)

Hung in the Academy as an object of beauty, playing second fiddle in worship of her husband—Crewe's account of his wife is the most conventional middle-class view of women. All Crewe's vigour revolves around himself. Gissing reinforces this by his relationship with Beatrice French. Beatrice is vigorous, his equal and desperately in love with him—but he calls her "old chap" all the time. To him she is a man and he cannot imagine any other kind of relationship with her. Admittedly Gissing endorses this (Beatrice's dietary preferences are wheeled out to show it) but this does not detract from the contradiction. At the top of the Monument there is an observation platform. And the movement from observation platform to front window is not so hard to imagine.

Nancy is never allowed to see Crewe in this way. His image just collapses with the superior physical attraction of Tarrant, and he is displaced just because she feels herself in control of the situation with him, whereas she feels overwhelmed by Tarrant who elicits "the more ambitious desire" and at the same time threatens her self-confidence. The contrast is more explicit in ideological terms when Tarrant asks her how she likes the advertisements on Teignmouth pier. She replies that she sees no harm in them and he sardonically replies "You like the world as it is? There's wisdom in that. Better be in harmony with one's time, advertisements and all" (II, iv). Tarrant offers more ambition because Crewe offers her only harmony, control, the dead routine of the suburb. The Jubilee is the way back to the suburb, the image of what made it, the image that will keep it ticking over.

3

We can certainly account for the development of the novel in this way, but we can't help being disappointed that Nancy is never allowed to work out her relationship with Crewe and is never brought to face the contradictions it implies. Added to which, as Adrian Poole implies, Tarrant is a bore. Detached and articulate he becomes a mouthpiece of various ideas about modern suburban marriage (hugger-mugger marriage as he calls it), the absurdity of two people living all the time together, the source of the servant problem, and so on—ideas which are much more adequately dramatised in the French/Peachey sections. Unlike most of Gissing's exponent characters, he is never really gripped by circumstances—whatever suffering he undergoes is off-stage. So he acts and speaks like a cynical decadent whose unconventionality is only an expedient of his own egoism: "Infidelity in a woman is much worse than in a man" (VI, iii)—you can't be more despicably conventional than that. What makes it worse is that the authorial perspective on Tarrant seems so shaky. His specious intellectual sophistication, the Hodiernals, the banal facts he produces to keep Nancy in her place, like the fact that Keats was once at Teignmouth, is never really placed. And yet intelligence plays very little part in the way he reacts. Thus, for example, when Nancy sends him money, implying that he needs her to keep him, we get this:

> His first sensation was one of painful surprise; thereupon succeeded fiery resentment. Reason put in a modest word, hinting that he had deserved no better; but he refused to listen. Nothing could excuse so gross an insult. He had not thought Nancy capable of this behaviour. Tested, she betrayed the vice of birth. Her imputation upon his motive to marrying her was sheer vulgar abuse, possible only on vulgar lips. Well and good; now he knew her; all the torment of conscience he had suffered was needless.
>
> (V, v)

We note how moral questions become reduced to a vocabulary of temperament. Against the argument of "reason" there is "fiery resentment". What excuses Tarrant from the fact that he has seduced Nancy without loving her, married her with resentment, abandoned her to a life of hypocrisy and constraint, is that she is "vulgar" in her abuse. Tarrant seems to cry out either for Meredith or George Eliot, the most effective analysts of male egoism. But Gissing isn't up to that. His male egoist can only be dealt with by the woman he destroys—and she is in no position to place him where he should be placed. Gissing's prose here betrays his total lack of aesthetic distance. The retreat to words like resentment, insult, vice of birth, is a retreat from the text and its implications.

Having said this, however, it is possible to claim that the Nancy-Tarrant relationship belongs with the suburban theme as much as any other. In fact, of course, it is obvious that the Peachey marriage is a mirror image of the Tarrant marriage and that Arthur's decision to break with his wife is a kind of inarticulate version of Tarrant's "sincerity". Equally, on the other side, the Horace/Fanny affair is a reflection of the seduction theme. Both seem to vindicate Tarrant—the suburban wife and the suburban whore are the projections of womanhood that he avoids. However, the values with which he resists are more complex than the mere aristocratic temperament we see in that passage just quoted. When Nancy talks with him at Champion Hill, Tarrant is already talking about making money out of the Bahamas, and though this doesn't work out, it is of a piece with what is certainly a submerged motive in his character: "How would the strong, unscrupulous, really ambitious man act in such a case" (V, iv). Much of Tarrant's personality, both the sexual process and the cold insistence on liberty and travel, has what seems like an imperialist-social Darwinian "integrity". Over and above the aestheticism is a commitment to self which entails conquest, and it is certainly through conquest that he attains and ultimately commands Nancy. Actually the way in which their relationship works out resembles the story of Peachey's marriage as much as it contrasts with it. After Arthur Peachey has left home, there is a vividly ironic sense in the respectable stucco villa in which the French sisters physically set about one another: "the last ray of pseudo-civilisation was rent off these young women" (IV, v.) Significantly, it is Beatrice who wins it, and it is Beatrice who survives. And this is reflected in the Nancy-Tarrant relationship: essentially Nancy gives way to Tarrant because he is stronger than her. When he pleads for forgiveness, she can resist him, but as he sticks rigidly to his plan of seeing her from time to time while he lives apart, she begins to accept her role. No work for her, no independence. Women as he says must be "above the scrummage". But Nancy accepts this not rationally, rather in Darwinian terms:

177

One thought that troubles me is, that every generation of women is sacrificed to the generation that follows; and of course that's why women are so inferior to men. But then again Nature says that women are born *only* to be sacrificed. I always come round to that. I don't like it, but I am bound to believe it.

(VI, iii)

Later Tarrant simply says, "I am your superior in *force* of mind and *force* of body" (my italics). What this rationalises, ironically, is not, as Gissing seems to have intended, an "amazing marriage", but merely the logical consequence of the suburban "natural" relationship: the man free to roam in search of money; the woman submitting to the sacrifice of herself to future generations. The most loving remark she can make is "I won't stand in your way". The ultimate, unintended irony is that Tarrant tells Nancy to find herself a house "in the western suburbs". Thus the novel seems to collapse precisely into the contradictions it exposes. On this basis we can't help feeling a sneaking sympathy for the French sisters who have too much animal lust to be kept in their suburban places. I certainly don't think Gissing faces this possibility. But, as so often, he can really only bring the novel to heel by hemming in the protagonist not with circumstance but with fictional contingencies which make it impossible for him or her to have any choice. What happens, however, in the process is that the ideological bases of the final "virtue of necessity" are exposed and unassimilated.

In that passage which I have just quoted, Nancy is speaking about "Nature". What is this nature that precipitates her towards seduction and betrayal? Basically it is a holiday in Teignmouth—the suburban conquest of the unlabouring world, the enclave of the resort. Tarrant himself is capable of making "nature" his ally in the seduction of Nancy and equally capable of cursing it for landing him in a trap. Nancy has been offered two versions of pastoral—the Monument and the Resort, commerce and culture which stand apart from but are part of the suburban routine. She begins to resist the illusions just as Tarrant returns from abroad; in the same chapter she arranges to take a job with Beatrice French. And she can face him with a very powerful realism:

"I wonder how I had the heart to leave you alone."

Nancy raised herself, and said coldly: "It was what I might have expected. I had only my own folly to thank. You behaved as most men would."

This was a harder reproach than any yet. Tarrant winced under it. He would much rather have been accused of abnormal villainy.

(V, iii)

The whole scene has this gritty quality. Tarrant's egoism is ripped open by Nancy's cold recognition of the real explorative nature of his seduction (and sending him a banknote is a proper response to the way he is). Despite Gissing's attempts to make him an outsider, he is as conventional as Nancy implies here. And this is what the novel finally can't take. Peachey, Crewe, Barmby, Tarrant, they are all in their different ways suburban deities whose conventionality is revealed at the point of sexual politics. But that is because the suburbs do reveal themselves at that point. Space, greenery, retreat—they constitute not the life of man but an elaborate bed where he can sleep in the passive compliant arms of his mother-whore Academy picture. Gissing set out to write about suburban London in the year of the Jubilee. He creates a fiction which does not hold together because he cannot allow the questions he raises to be put at the root of the social system. Instead he wants to portray a superficial disgust—the suburb as veneer, "respectable brass curtain-rodded skies" (VI, iii). Yet it is in the unresolved tensions, the unexplained gaps in the narrative—why Nancy finally accepts Tarrant, what nature it is that insists on keeping her quiet in the western suburbs—that he exposes what underlies the "veneer" and its apparent other side. What underlies it is the capitalist system itself. The dream is a product, but the process which makes it possible is a continuing, revolving, frustrated energy called a market. It is not surprising that Tarrant doesn't want to read Nancy's novel. It would indeed involve her in the scrummage, but it would also have in it the "scrummage" she has been involved in. The roads out of the suburb are the roads back. Not the odd women this time, but all the women, lawless prisoners of the division of labour and the contradiction of the bourgeois dream.

179

NOTE

1 See Dyos, *Victorian Suburb: A Study of the Growth of Camberwell* (Leicester, 1961). I have drawn on this book a good deal for this chapter.

7

Conclusion

1

The major novels of the early 'nineties appeared regularly at the rate of one a year, each of them in three-volume form. In 1894, the three-decker was officially dead, and this seems to have had its effect on Gissing's literary output. For there is a three-year gap between *In the Year of the Jubilee* and his next important novel, *The Whirlpool*. Not that Gissing was unproductive: in 1895, he published twenty-six short stories, *Eve's Ransom*, *The Paying Guest* and *Sleeping Fires*, and in 1896 a much revised version of *The Unclassed* and many more stories. These are also the years of Gissing's recognition—the visit to Meredith at Box Hill and to Hardy at Max Gate, the friendship with Wells, even the great flattery of the Reverend Jay Osborne's plagiarism of *The Nether World*. But at the same time there is also an un-doubted trivialisation in his work which is continued beyond *The Whirlpool* in the lightweight fiction of his last years—*The Town Traveller*, *Our Friend The Charlatan* and *Will Warburton*. It is as though the pressure of writing three-deckers every year was a determining condition not only for the length of his stories, but also for their intensity. Gissing's stories are often shrewd and lively, but they come all too easily, like a plague of life's little ironies, and his propensity for comedy in these years makes it seem as though he was beginning to imitate his more trivial imitators of the 'nineties. And yet we cannot simply dismiss the last ten years of his career as a decline. *The Whirlpool* is one of his most achieved novels, and these are the years that produced the books on Dickens. What we have to deal with rather is what effectively constitutes a new phase in his writing which takes off from *In the Year of the Jubilee*.

I ended my account of that novel by suggesting that in his portrayal of the consumer zone of the urban society, the suburb, Gissing reveals what motivates the market as the restless energy and thwarted desire of the middle-class wife. Most of his novels up to that point portray the exhaustion of energy by the city, but *In the Year of the Jubilee* is not about exhaustion; rather it is about the forms of repression which never properly work. The short novel which follows it, *Eve's Ransom*, registers this uncontainable energy. It is an odd novel, moving between Birmingham and London, with intervals of Paris, having, at its centre, a girl who is from the Midlands but who "belongs" essentially (as an immigrant always especially belongs to a city) to London. The detailed topography of the midland city, named, like Gissing's London, but characteristically nearly always in darkness and with a sense of total isolation, is measured against the fleeting and crowded zone around Gower Street. In the first, Eve's picture, static, like an idea—in the second, Eve herself constantly disappearing, indecisive, casual. Hilliard tries to buy her and set her up in a steady life, moving her first to Paris and then back to Birmingham. But he is fascinated by what he can't contain. What is important here is that this is a novel about urban energy, not repressed as in *In the Year of the Jubilee*, but ultimately irrepressible. You can't fix Eve in the suburbs, because she is a creature of the metropolis. We might feel the novel to be lightweight. Certainly it seems only to be a fragment of a much more serious novel about the industrial city that Gissing planned, but it is equally a short effective statement of what he is trying to define which he hasn't engaged with previously, and much of the minor work—*The Paying Guest, The Town Traveller* for example—is trying to do the same thing: to find a form which will urbanise not oppression but vitality. *The Whirlpool* is the nearest he comes to do this, and in doing it, he achieves a remarkable fiction about the hegemonic world of the metropolitan nineties.

2

The Whirlpool is a new kind of title for Gissing. It immediately draws attention to a condition of life: "Was he himself to become a victim of this social disease? Was he, resistless, to be drawn into the muddy whirlpool, to spin round and round among gibbering phantoms, abandoning himself with a grin of inane conceit, or clutching in desperation at futile hopes?" (II, vii). "Social disease" gives this title-word the same status as "The Waste Land": it is a mythic image denoting a modern cultural situation, at the same time as being a specific landscape. Earlier in the novel, a discussion between the hero and his friend Mrs. Abbot (herself widowed by the whirlpool of speculation) makes the nature of the social disease clear. Rolfe has said that there is no time for the proper upbringing of children, "especially so if you live in a whirlpool", and his interlocutor replies:

"Yes, I know it too well, the whirlpool way of life," said Mrs. Abbott, her eyes on the far-off mountains. "I know how easily one is drawn into it. It isn't only idle people." "Of course not. There's the Whirlpool of the furiously busy. Round and round they go; brains humming till they melt or explode."

(II, ii)

The image is carefully worked out. The whirlpool way of life is defined against the "far-off mountains"—the social illusion against the intractable silence of the natural world. But if it is phantasmal, it is also irresistible because it is a condition of social living—the way we live now. This condition is juxtaposed, however, not only against nature, but also against a lost world of human values: "when there's no leisure, no meditation, no peace and no quietness . . ." And that is why it is important that the theme should be introduced in the context of children—it concerns the breakdown of family life, the destruction of domesticity. The Whirlpool is about many things, but what is central is the disruption of the home by the social roundabout.

The image congeals the many levels of this disruption. The novel is set in motion by a financial crash which makes widows of wives and émigrés of fallen rentiers. Financial speculation and its precariousness recurs through the novel like a persistent itch, and it is both what domesticity depends on and is threatened by. The whirlpool of high capitalism then, but equally the whirlpool of metropolitan culture—the round of concerts, hit shows,

183

agents and soirées, touching the demi-monde. Beyond this it is the whirlpool of modernity, of a new ethic, emancipated, tolerant, subjective, which throws all assumptions into the melting-pot. And above all, the image conjures up the place itself, the metropolis, the bustling outside, crowded and confused, within which or against which one has to contrive a privacy. The novel is an updated version of *The Way We Live Now*, but the constant reference back to the question of the children should remind us that it is strictly contemporary with James's most searching portrayal of the rentier world of London in the 'nineties, *The Awkward Age*. The image of the Whirlpool itself with its accreted references, and its effect on the private life, is very much an image for its time.

The sense of an age, of "now", is not incidental or even merely supportive—it is the *raison d'être* of the novel. Modernity is the novel's dominant motif. Rolfe and Carnaby are introduced as both "impressively modern"—in everything a contrast with one another, but drawn together by precisely their modernity. Alma castigates her stepmother for talking in "that early Victorian way" (a phrase which echoes her mentor's comment on her husband's concern with simpler morality). There are persistent reminders that we are in a late Victorian world. Thus "boom" for example is mentioned as a new word. At the end of the novel Rolfe is enjoying *Barrack Room Ballads* which first appeared in 1892. Both Rolfe and Carnaby are involved in commerce which is new and in which new advances were at that time made, Rolfe in photography (Eastman produced the Kodak box camera in 1888, and Rolfe is concerned with marketing a new hand camera), Carnaby in cycles (Dunlop had invented pneumatic tyres in 1889). This is not merely a matter of local detail. Photography and cycling are significant features of the development of communications. The cycle is to create mass urban mobility—the photograph to be the source of total revolution in the media. Curiously, Gissing seems to offer these as positive forms of commitment for his otherwise *desoeuvré* heroes. And against them the pseudo-Bohemian world of Alma, Rolfe's wife, is limited and static. But I think that this is part of the inevitability of the Whirlpool: you can find interesting things to do in it but it is still not the world at one with the far-off mountains. On the contrary, it is, in effect, a further extension of the Whirlpool. The cycle, for example, is instrumental in the urbanisation of the countryside —making it more accessible, and therefore more geared to urban leisure needs. What is most obviously important, however, about these historical details is that Gissing is concerned to locate his story in a specific time by images which indicate its new and forward pointing forces. "Boom" is a word that belongs to a new intensification of marketing process for the arts. Kipling's work (especially *Barrack Room Ballads*) is the high point of middlebrow literature. The innovations are culturally decisive. *The Whirlpool* is a historical novel in the sense that it reproduces a phase in English life, but its history is inscribed as the history of the coming race. Hence the emphasis on children and education, on how to prepare for the future.

The modernity of the novel is reflected in the pervasive representation of an ideological formation responsive to this newness. At the root of it is a way of seeing which is best identified as social Darwinism. This in turn is reproduced as specific ideologies —Imperialism on the one hand as a potential ethical response, and on the other, a "counter" ideology which we may identify as Decadence. However sharply opposed the characters in the novel are, they are all contained within this formation. Nobody poses values which can countervail it. The "real" Whirlpool is that created by the boundaries of vision in which the novel is contained.

We have noticed in previous novels the presence of Darwinian or pseudo-Darwinian norms, but in this work there is a systematic attempt to come to terms with them. The story starts in 1885 with the collapse of the Britannia Loan Company and it is precisely in that year that Herbert Spencer published *Man Versus the State*, his most lucid rationalisation of a free capitalist ethic based on the assumption that social action could only impede the "natural" law of the survival of the fittest and that therefore any attempt to rectify natural processes of selection—physiological or economic—was an unwarrantable interference which could only intensify the operation of that law by appearing to delay it. Social Darwinism at its crudest carried Darwin's discovery of the law of natural selection (simplified in the sixth edition of *The Origin of Species* by the adoption of Spencer's phrase "survival of the

185

fittest") direct into the social life of human beings. Rolfe himself announces this perspective early in the novel:

> People snivel over the deaths of babies; I see nothing to grieve about. If a child dies, why, the probabilities are that it *ought* to die; if it lives, it lives, and you get survival of the fittest.
>
> (I, ii)

Later we are told that "Circumstance at this stage of his career, was Harvey's god; he waited upon its direction with an air of wisdom, of mature philosophy" (I, iii) and when the Britannia loan company fails, he applies this wisdom:

> After all, it promised to clear the air. These explosions were periodic, inevitable, wholesome . . . This is how mankind progresses. Harvey Rolfe felt glad that no theological or scientific dogma constrained him to a justification of the laws of life.
>
> (I, v)

and when he is confronted with his wife's short lived enthusiasms he is "vexed rather than surprised . . . For about this time he was reading and musing much on questions of heredity" (II, i). Other characters rationalise in the same way—Alma, we are told:

> rebelled against the fate which made her life dishonourable. Fate, she declared, not the depravity of her own heart. From the dark day that saw her father's ruin, she had been condemned to a struggle with circumstances.
>
> (III, ix)

and Carnaby, though he takes the blame for the murder he commits, explains it away in deterministic terms:

> It's all my cursed fault—just because I'm a fierce, strong brute, who ought to be anywhere but among civilised people.
>
> (II, xiii)

These statements vary a good deal from one another—the degree of determinism, the various ascriptions of effects to circumstance and temperament (and heredity) do not add up to a systematic ideology. But they all belong within a system which allots ethical and social questions to an area of self-justifying fact. Survival means adaptation rather than change: right action becomes a matter of making the right kind of pact with one's inherited self and one's unalterable circumstances. Carnaby makes the right choice when he goes to Australia and does badly when he sacrifices the need to be in touch with primitive living to his wife's need to be with civilised (i.e. late Victorian) people. Alma makes a series of wrong choices to escape her own limitations and ultimately is destroyed by her own psychological breakdown. Rolfe, wiser than either and to that extent more lost amid the limited range of questions he is allowed to put, effectively gives up life as an end in itself and vests everything in the future through children.

His child becomes the main term of his pact with life. Throughout the first part Rolfe is largely a passive intellectual gossip whose own life is irreproachable and pointless. His marriage makes no essential difference to this—retreat becomes more structured, the aimless passivity of his life more "traditional" (a word he uses about his own role as a husband). And when this breaks down, he is left gazing into the future through his little boy:

> Fruitless? There sounded from somewhere in the house a shrill little cry, arresting his thought, and controverting it without a syllable. Nay, fruitless his life could not be, if his child grew up. Only the chosen few, the infinitesimal minority of mankind, leave spiritual offspring, or set their single mark upon the earth; the multitude are but parents of a new generation, live but to perpetuate the race. It is the will of nature, the common lot.
>
> (II, i)

Much later in the novel, this resigned compromise yields a moment of tenderness and love rare in Gissing and potentially full of radical hope. He feels an infinite pathos for the vulnerable child to whom he is "the giver of life and for that dread gift must hold himself responsible" (III, vi). The father is the child's God, and it is only because of the distorted religion which "under direst penalties exacts from groaning and travailing humanity a tribute of fear and love to the imagined Author of its being" that the "duty of children to parents" is stressed at the expense of the far more "immense debt" due from father to trusting son.

This is potentially not merely tender but also radical. It commits the father to trying to make a better world and it demystifies the family without turning from it in Malthusian disgust. But the ideological limitation within which Rolfe's insight is contained is clear both in the line of thought that he has travelled and in the relation of the child-father relationship to the novel as a whole. At the beginning when Rolfe is voicing a crude Darwinism, he makes an equally radical but opposite point: "Most wives are sacrificed to the next generation—an outrageous absurdity" (I, ii). To move from this to a conception of the awesome duties of parenthood is a straight road to traditional values. More importantly, the father-child relationship in the novel is not really a part of its plot—it is rather a normative distraction which lies outside the main events and enables Rolfe to avoid facing up to his marriage and what its tensions mean. He sees what is happening to Alma, but he simply judges her neuroses and her ennui in terms of her lack of interest in the child. It enables him to look on her with passive moral shock. It is as though he has forgotten his statement about wives being sacrificed to the next generation, whereas a truly radical position would have been an attempt to face up to the contradiction between the "outrageous absurdity" of sacrifice and the "immense debt" entailed by giving life. It would also have made for a more satisfactory novel because Rolfe would have had to enter the story instead of complacently watching and judging. The "will of nature" supplies an outside, a beyond like the far-off mountains, by which the unanswerable questions posed by marriage are avoided.

But Rolfe's retreat into ideology takes another, more topical form. At the beginning of the novel, he announces his own Imperialist fervour:

> We're rotting at home—some of us sunk in barbarism, some coddling themselves in over-refinement. What's the use of preaching peace and civilisation, when we know that England's just beginning her big fight.

> (I, ii)

This is elaborated with brutal extremism: "We shall fight like blazes in the twentieth century. It's the only thing that keeps Englishmen sound . . . War is England's banking." It is a vision of total domination—"We have to swallow the whole, of course". And he actually speaks of "a reaction of wholesome barbarism".

It has all the makings of a fascist position (which, of course, was latent in Imperialism). The subject seems to be dropped—so much of Rolfe's rhetoric at the beginning of the novel is belied by his marriage—but it is reiterated again at the end, when Alma is safely dead and Rolfe is left alone with the child. He praises *Barrack Room Ballads* because in it is "the strong man made articulate" and he goes on to say, "Mankind won't stand it much longer, this encroachment of the humane spirit" and looks forward to the day when we may see "our boys blown into small bits by the explosive that hasn't got its name yet". The rhetoric is accurate enough. Rolfe echoes the commonplace degeneracy theme which was common to social Darwinism and to Imperialism —over-civilisation needs to be met by "a stouter race". Sport, war and conquest contain the brutal but healthy future. Equally Rolfe passingly recognises the true economic basis of British Imperialism: "We can't make money quite so easily as we used to; scoundrels in Germany and elsewhere have dared to learn the trick of commerce." Imperialism became more than a moral piety because Britain was being defeated in industrial capitalism by the superior technology and organisation of Prussia and the United States. It needed therefore to find new areas for the exploitation of raw materials and the fabrication of easily controlled markets.

What we have to ask, however, is what this rhetoric has to do with the novel as a whole. And we ought to be aware that conservative as he was, Gissing himself hated both Imperialism and war, so putting it in the mouth of his apparently exponent character is likely to make for complications. Rolfe himself, of course, is very much an armchair Imperialist and an ironic distance is established by the way in which he brings it to bear on the world he sees. What he does see is that "we are rotting at home". Imperialism, like his far-off mountains, like the metaphysic of paternity, is a way out of the Whirlpool. But it is for others, for the future—for him still the study and the mountains, though they crumble under the pressure of his life-style. Equally the others do not live up to the ideology. Hugh Carnaby, who is robust, out of place in civilisation and who emigrates, is nothing like a full-blooded Imperialist: "something more of repose, of self-possession, and a slightly more intellectual brow, would have made him the best type of conquering, civilising Briton" (I, ii). If he is not quite up to it, neither is he properly committed: he is amused by Rolfe's jingoism and he treats his own desire to find a war in South Africa to satisfy him as a joke—"Nigger-hunting: superior big game". More importantly, Rolfe's Imperialism is aimed at the next generation: he first announces his theory in the context of what he would do if he had a son, and in the final chapter, when he is yelling his approval of Kipling, he is playing the part essentially of the father. But little Hugh is not even like his namesake. After all the talk about athletics and war, his friend Morton looks at the child: "slight, with little or no colour in his cheeks, a wistful, timid smile on the too intelligent cheeks". The Imperialism is a relevant topical response to the Whirlpool, it is an ideology meant to meet the present with the future. But it is just an ideology, another world to look at and seek comfort from. More significantly it has to do with domination. Both Rolfe and Carnaby seek domination, but that is only because they are dominated—by their wives.

Alma Rolfe and Sybil Carnaby are as modern as their husbands, and this means that they are contained within the same year of seeing things. But they are at the other end of the ideological pavilion. Sybil's comment that Hugh is "rather early Victorian", which is echoed by Alma later, place them in the highly civilised aesthetic world of the 'nineties: "Art is art—and all these other things have nothing whatever to do with it." When Alma questions Rolfe about their marriage—"Are we talking on equal terms, or is it master and servant" (III, iii)—his reply is "Husband and wife, Alma, that is all". The question at issue is her "professional career" and the career is specifically located in the world of artistic production. Thus although it is one of sexual equality generally, it is more specifically one of the "new woman". Alma's career puts her in touch with an oppositional ideology which is not as fully voiced as that of Rolfe's Imperialism, but is never-the less present as a social force which motivates the plot more actively than Rolfe's ideas. This oppositional ideology is Darwinian insofar as it results in an admiration for subjectivity (denoting force) and a commitment to moral relativity. The major spokesman for it is the sly millionaire and patron Cyrus Redgrave. Early on, he announces himself as a pseudo-Bohemian:

190

I have seen much of artists; known them intimately, and studied their lives. One and all, they date their success from some passionate experience. From a cold and conventional existence can come nothing but a cold and conventional art.

(I, viii)

and he comes much closer to a Paterian view of things when he compliments and "places" Alma in a discussion of Hugh Carnaby's primitivism with which she cannot sympathise:

"Perhaps because you yourself represent civilisation in its subtlest phase, and when I am with you I naturally think only of that, I don't say I would have thriven as a backwoodsman; but I admire the type in Carnaby. That is one of *our* privileges, don't you think? We live in imagination quite as much as in everyday existence. You, I am sure, are in sympathy with infinite forms of life—and," he added, just above his breath, "you could realise so many of them."

(II, ix)

The idea that civilisation is classifiable in "phases" and that different "types" belong to different phases of it is central to Pater's thought: it recognises historical change and makes possible its spatialisation by evolutionary theory. But equally Paterian is the point that living in imagination makes possible sympathy with infinite *forms* of life, and the concept that the individual "realises" those forms. It is a way of thinking that underlies the aesthetic concept of style, and its concomitant, moral relativism. So it is not merely that Alma moves towards a life of artistic success (with the stress on performance rather than production) but also that it entails her in a socially modish version of aesthetic ideology. It is interesting that music, to which all the arts, in Pater's view, aspire, should be the centre of this social circle and that the stress, whenever it is discussed, should be on tonality and interpretation.

The tension between two ideological worlds—the primitivist and the decadent—is the basis of the novel's modernity. But characteristically it is brought to bear on a very specific and secular issue—how are we to live? What kind of *structure* makes for peace and fulfilment? The novel is about domesticity and what in modern life threatens it, and the two sets of values present themselves as ways of looking outwards from this question. If we sometimes feel that the action of the novel is divorced from the discussion that goes on in it, it is not because Gissing can't bring together the flow of ideas and the central motif— it is rather because the world in which the question has to be put settles nothing. The home locates itself between the mountains and the salon, and neither gives it any form. Although Gissing seems to have broken with the urbanism of his earlier fiction, making a contrast between the lodging world of the Whirlpool itself and the house in North Wales, the contrast is not really between the city and the country. The "country" home offers, in fact, a highly urban and modern accommodation:

> Nor did the equipment of the room differ greatly from what is usual in middle class houses. The clock on the mantelpiece was flanked with bronzes; engravings and autotypes hung about the walls; door and window had their appropriate curtaining; the oak sideboard shone with requisite silver. Everything unpretentious; but no essential of comfort, as commonly understood, seemed to be lacking.

(II, i)

It is a very interesting passage in itself: "essential of comfort" is a phrase summing up what in fact are luxuries—ornaments, bronzes, engravings, curtains, silver. Walter Benjamin stresses that the great change in interiors in the nineteenth century came when the home was sharply differentiated from the place of work. The interior shuts out work and also "social concerns" (*Charles Baudelaire*, p. 167) and thus it creates within it a world of illusion. It is both the private citizen's universe and his casing— traces of living encapsulated in the decor. *Art nouveau*, which began to dominate design at the end of the century, broke up this private theatre box through the use of new materials and designs drawn from naked Nature to confront the technologically armed environment. The Rolfes' interior is still the Victorian private universe. It is removed not only from the innovations of design but also the rustic functionalism of the farm-house or cottage. North Wales itself is not so much a place—an environment—as a distance, the furthest possible from the centre. When Rolfe complains that domestic life is played out, when we are told that domestic matters are a trial to his nerves, when he agrees with Alma that it is no crime "if women hate the bother and misery of housekeeping" (I, v), it is because he is moving towards this very static sense of domestic comfort. It is one that is the more oppressive because he has no place of work to go to which might appear to justify it. But it is an essentially urban ideal. North Wales is like a very far-flung suburb. And the problems remain of what to do with this comfort.

For Rolfe himself, his eyes on the mountains, the Empire and the future, there is no problem. The theatre of the middle-class living room is merely the intensification of his passive distance from life itself. This distance is to lose focus as he moves to the actual suburbs; his concentration begins to go and he begins to look forward to going to the photography shop as a place of work. But this is only trivial compared with what happens to Alma. She soon recognises that "marriage had signified her defeat, the end of high promises, brave aspirations" (II, iv). The middle section of the novel traces very effectively the psychology of her oppression—energetic and lethargic by starts, taking up different enthusiasms, suffering from unspecified illnesses, Alma is an early version of the bored wife. At the same time she is a very dominant personality:

> he spoke with effort, vainly struggling against that peculiar force of Alma's personality which had long ago subdued him.
>
> (II, viii)

He retreats behind his own passivity, keeping silent in the face of Alma's neurotic energies, and when he does assert himself in the traditional role of husband it is with the explicit recognition that the traditional is not the primitive: "for I believe there was a time when primitive women had the making of man in every sense, and somehow knocked a few ideas into his head" (III, iii). Alma is both highly modern and at the same time has simply unfocussed energies. Rolfe's middle way of domestic inertia has no place for a woman. What she is left, once she gets back to London, is a life of petty jealousies and mild flirtations; finally of narcotics. Rolfe's role here is recognisably inadequate. On the one hand he is contented with a life which leaves her out of account. On the other, when he is aware of this, he makes no attempt to influence her and leaves to her "an entire responsibility" (II, iii). It is not confronted or shared. Alma is left to survive on her own. Rolfe's interventions are restricted by his determinism. The result is that we have a double sense of this novel. On the one hand it has a highly melodramatic plot in the second section which ends with the manslaughter of Redgrave by Carnaby who mistakenly supposes Alma is his wife at a tryst. On the other hand, the novel drifts, after this climax, into plotlessness as the day-to-day life of the Rolfes becomes increasingly vexed and pointless. I think that in some ways this is true to the tension that Gissing has set up. Two incompatible people, one with energy drawn towards the treacherous pseudo-aesthetic world of the Whirlpool, almost needing to live on intrigue and ambiguity, frenziedly pursuing mild professional success with its need for agents, publicity and patronages, and the other gazing wistfully on the outside world from within the comfortable middle-class armchair—the plotting and the plotless. For neither is there any organic reality, for neither any possibility of working out a relationship. At the same time, it is clear that Gissing is trying to cope with a situation for which he can find no objective correlative. The real struggle between Alma and Rolfe lies beneath the conscious issue of what kind of day-to-day structure a marriage should have. Neurosis is not rational, cannot be contained with rational detachment, especially when that detachment is limited to the social determinism which leaves forces to work themselves out. Innocence is the exception—lawlessness the rule: Alma's confused and contradictory sense of the world she moves in applies to the whole novel. The rule of lawlessness makes sense only in a world where "innocence" is contrived by the illusions of domesticity. A later writer will find a larger form to encounter the rule of lawlessness and uncover its energies in a way which the ideology cannot merely defuse. Gissing is not Lawrence, but in a way he needed to be to write this novel. But The Whirlpool has its own eccentric effectiveness. For without Rolfe's timid retreat into the norms of bronze statuettes we would not see the discomfiting effects of comforts—the need that middle-class peace makes for its own frenzied whirlpool. Rolfe's Imperialism is disgusting, but what truly places it is that he cannot see that rotting at home is not merely a national disease, but also a private and

personal one. The fighting future he wants for his son is reactionary, partly because it is at the cost of the fighting present his
wife needs. Rolfe is Gissing's most foolish protagonist and *The
Whirlpool*, because of this, in many ways, his most disturbing
novel. The way we live now is the way we have made and go on
making.

3

The novels which immediately follow *The Whirlpool*, *The
Crown of Life* and *Our Friend The Charlatan*, make explicitly
clear Gissing's dislike of Imperialism and social Darwinism, but
they only confirm what emerges from *The Whirlpool* and earlier
novels—that Gissing's ideological position, by which I mean not
his "beliefs" but the terms in which he can put questions to what
he sees, allow him only to oppose such developments without in
the end re-forming his fictional method in such a way that they
could be fully dramatised and therefore exposed. Social Darwinism and theoretical Imperialism are both ideological rationalisations of psychological and social processes that are inaccessible
to "humane" values. And Gissing's own ideology can only retreat
to humane values. That is why *The Private Papers of Henry Ryecroft* turns out to be a better fiction than the novels which try
to represent what it is in retreat from. For this text, as I have
tried to show, reflects not the forces that make for the defeat of
those values, but, on the contrary, the values *in retreat*, preserved
therefore in a mode of what Adrian Poole has termed, "voluptu-
ous relaxation" (p. 207), but with the conditions of that preservation visible. All the *novels* of these late years contain uneasy
representations of that thwarted energy visible in the pose of
Nancy Lord as she looks out of her father's window, and that
unacceptable vulgar joy in which she momentarily finds her objective correlative which emanates from Luckworth Crewe. Even so
slight a work as *The Town Traveller* has this energy held at than uneasy comic distance. But although, at least in *Eve's Ransom* and
The Whirlpool, Gissing finds way of dramatising this energy, the
structure of the novel itself cannot see anything but its calamit-
ousness, because the only register of their effect, the bewildered,
even foolish narrative centre, can only bring a rational understand-

ing which, in the case of Rolfe, collapses finally into the available rationalisations which end up by denying precisely the rationality which is under threat.

I made the comparison with Lawrence not casually but precisely because what is new in Gissing's fiction after *In the Year of the Jubilee* is this sense of a civilisation rotting from within because it can only contain the "irrational" in ideologies which deny its values in the cause of the institutions through which it practises those values. In the major novels of the early 'nineties, Gissing is primarily concerned with the material determinants which throw up these ideologies. These determinants are registered through social groups who are trapped in them. It is when he begins to concern himself with groups that are *ideologically* as opposed to *economically* conditioned by these determinants that he suddenly seems to engage with what is more familiar to the privileged public of literature as modern life—the Whirlpool, the coming man. To put it simply, whereas urbanisation is the trap of the unclassed, the trap of the dominant class in civilisation itself and its discontents. Of course, as *In the Year of the Jubilee* and *The Whirlpool* (and, in a different way *Eve's Ransom* and *The Paying Guest*) show, this is still deeply bound up for Gissing with the urbanisation which is the domain of all his fiction. It is simply an extension into the prosperous suburbs. A teleological way of describing Gissing's career would be to say that he travels from Clerkenwell to Gunnersbury, moves across the social space of the city, from the ghetto to the lodging-house to the villa, and that as he moves in this direction, he increasingly locates the determinations of late capitalism in the "free" subjectivity. Sidney Kirkwood is depressed because his life is depressing; Reardon and the characters in *The Odd Women* are depressed or frustrated because they live in an ambiguous zone which disables them from the kind of life which would make survival worth having; Nancy Lord and Alma Rolfe are frustrated because they cannot accommodate their desires in the prosperity that is available. That is why Gissing in his last phase seems more and more to be a failed forerunner of Lawrence, for Lawrence more than any novelist produces texts which account for those unaccommodated energies which explain the determinations of "free" choice. Gissing is most true to himself when that freedom is restricted to a choice between surviving in a hostile world by becoming one of the enemy, or being destroyed in a hopeless effort not to give in.

It is necessary to pursue this contrast further in order to see why it is that while it is accurate to define Gissing's development in terms which project him towards Lawrence, this is not the real basis of Gissing's importance. The fundamental ideological difference between Gissing and Lawrence is that Lawrence has from very early on his own way of questioning those energies which Gissing can only look at with bewilderment. The characters of Skrebensky and Gerald Crich are both motivated within an Imperialist and social Darwinian ideology. They represent the official violence of late capitalism, and yet they are both destroyed by what confronts them. For what confronts them is not an opposition but a knowledge which can take possession of them as objects of consumption—the knowledge inherited and learnt by the Brangwen sisters. And this knowledge is not formulated within the novel as an ideology. On the contrary, it is the very motivation of Lawrence's fiction, which is the same as saying that it is his own position within ideology itself. For Lawrence makes himself the artificer of that knowledge in the writing which breaks down, through syntax and image, the conscious fixity that is imposed on what he would think of as the unconscious: Ursula and Gudrun become the instruments of that knowledge. Alma makes Rolfe look foolish, but she never goes through him, just as he is never able to meet the energies that he confronts in her. There is only a polarisation into given positions—the decadence for her, Imperialism for him, the London scene for her, the cottage with views of the far-off mountains for him. There is no going into the far-off mountains to bring back a new knowledge and power. To put it more rigorously, there is no way in Gissing that the unconscious can be given voice: it can only exhibit itself as a grinning phantom, or be looked at with a worried eye.

When I speak of the "unconscious" here, I mean Lawrence's concept of the unconscious not Freud's, and that is why I say that Lawrence's strength in relation to Gissing's limitation is related to his own ideological situation. For Lawrence's version of the unconscious does not come from a scientific investigation; rather it derives from a derivation of evolutionary theory: that is, Haeckel's idea of a unified organic life which is continually individuating itself by fragmentation. Allusions to evolutionary theory occur at crucial moments in both *The Rainbow* and *Women In Love*, and it is because evolutionary theory is at the basis of knowledge in Lawrence that he is able to do much more than portray the violence of late capitalist ideology. As I have argued, both Imperialism and large scale capitalism rely heavily on social analogies drawn from evolutionary theory. Gissing deplores those analogies, but has nothing to offer in its place, so that deploring social Darwinism tends to be the same as deploring life (hence the lifelong loyalty to Schopenhauer). Lawrence, however, has access to another kind of analogy from evolutionary theory, an analogy which turns the social Darwinist rationalisations of the irrational into intellectual phantoms, by seeming to give voice to the irrational itself, not socially contained but socially disruptive. Essentially it makes available the unconscious as a version of pastoral: it becomes the site of the "organic". For Gissing, pastoral is only available to one who is at grass, to Ryecroft whose life is over: for those still in life, it is only possible to cringe in more or less comfort. That is why he can in the end seem so passive and conservative even when he is able to see through the debilitating passivity of his protagonists.

But this difference is not merely a difference of age or temperament. It is more importantly a difference in the kind of effectivity of the two writers. Gissing and Lawrence have a great deal in common in their social formation. Both came from industrial societies, and if Gissing was lower middle-class rather than working-class, Lawrence was on the edge of whatever kind of privilege that status confers. If Gissing's father was an educated and enlightened man, Lawrence's mother was sufficiently sophisticated to give him access to the rich provincial intellectual life which was available. Both made their way through the public education system, which both rejected. Both made the decisive move of their career when they went to London. But the differences begin there. London remains the domain of Gissing's fiction—he becomes the novelist of urbanisation. For Lawrence, London is only a formative phase. The decisive experience socially for Lawrence was not urbanisation but industrialisation. Urbanisation and industrialisation are both historically products of capitalism, but they are not identical. Industrialisation manifests itself most obviously as technology. That is why an ideological "tradition" to which Lawrence belongs develops in the nineteenth century which can be identified by the concept of "industrialism". "Industrialism" is the mask in which capitalism presents itself to the traditional intellectual, enabling him to deplore the oppressions of capitalism as though they were the oppressions caused by mechanisation. Industrialism presupposes the availability of pastoral, the alternative, organic "real" which questions the mechanised actuality. Urbanisation, however, is not an operative ideological concept in this way. It is the actual spatial structure of capitalism; since it embraces the ideological dialectic of the country and the city (in suburbs, parks and holidays), the pastoral alternative is enclosed within it, and therefore not available to the traditional intellectual, except as a form of retirement. Gissing too makes some attempt to belong to the tradition which provides Lawrence with the ideological base of his fiction, but his domain is one where that tradition gives no help. That is why the mountains remain so far-off, become helplessly reduced to views. The romantic totalities are suburban, and the modernist totalities are still undifferentiated from the crowded movement in the streets, so that Gissing historically is caught between two great affirmative movements, but what he is caught in is not a vacuum, a "transition"; rather it is the raw space unsheltered by the organic, the pastoral, which is the condition by which literature preserves its integrity while inserting itself into the dominant ideology. It makes for important limitations in Gissing's work which are exposed in *The Whirlpool* and *The Private Papers of Henry Ryecroft*, but it is also what constitutes the basis of his uniqueness—a uniqueness which, to be sure, is an important and early example of the kind of domain celebrated in some modern writers, but not writers who form any kind of central tradition. I think of Joyce's Dublin, Dreiser's Chicago, Richard Wright's New York, and it is significant that none of these writers is English. The only example I can think of in England is that of *The Clergyman's Daughter* and *Down and Out in Paris and London*. It is not a question of influence or shared values, but rather of the few writers who are truly metropolitan—who take the actual city as a fictional base, as a structured universe which can only be questioned from within itself by its system of distances and mobility.

I wrote this book because from the first time I read Gissing, I felt that he was a novelist who had his own disturbing effect, and I have tried to locate this effect not by translating the novels into more acceptable terms, but by trying to see what they actually are. Of course, I am not claiming that he wrote greater novels than, say, Dickens or Lawrence to whom I have compared him in order to situate him. What I am saying is that the best novels are significantly different from those writers, and that they share with James and Hardy the same combative integrity. But I am not merely trying to urge that he is worth reading. I have needed to write about him because he seems to me to be a writer who offers us an important lesson, a lesson which calls into question our assumptions about the nature and function of literature. For literature is an ideological institution—it is not the same thing as literary texts, which are commodities with various use-values, nor as literary production which is a form of intellectual labour with determined conditions. Literature is rather a given set of values, a limited set of questions which texts are made to yield. The values have possibilities of variation—you can even seem to have to choose between them to the extent that certain acknowledged successes in literature have to be rejected altogether. The most important institutional function of literature is its making of ideology. In fact, most teachers of literature would claim that the close analysis of literary texts liberates the student from ideological conditioning—frees him from the stock response. It is this claim which precisely constitutes the ideological function of literature, because it creates the very important illusion that choice is theoretically possible. Literature makes it possible to distance the need for social action by drawing a line between language and behaviour. It is not that literature does not have moral lessons which might influence one's behaviour, it is rather that by the play of language within the text (or more precisely within the reading of a text) the "true" reader learns to accept his own privilege, to pose questions not to his own life, but to life as a whole. The most revolutionary text can be immunised in this way, because in the study of the text as literature, the conditions of its production are obscured by its canonisation; it becomes a kind of gospel ripe for commentary—it reflects, represents, mobilises itself as an object. What it ceases to do is to intervene in the world of social action. Reading is a private affair and literature calls into being a group, an élite, a specialised section of traditional intellectuals who can convince themselves that they are not conquered by the dominant ideology (which is an important condition of its conquest).

Gissing writes novels which are far from revolutionary: on the contrary, they rehearse values which are ludicrous parodies of culturalist ideologies. Neither evidently do they have much claim as social interventions. It is precisely because of this that I feel Gissing calls into question the whole of literature. Terry Eagleton[1] has shown how the concept of organic form, which is the fundamental assumption of the teaching of literature, reflects what it appears to contest, the higher organisation of capitalism. Organic form is the means by which the traditional intellectual is made organic in Gramsci's sense. Gissing's commitment to the organic is so weak that as soon as we try to reorganise the text in terms of its value as literature, we find it depressing or defeatist. We also find it formally inorganic—a landscape that is not fictionalised, a protagonist that is not representative, a story which has no finality. Of course, this is only to state the reading situation negatively. What I have tried to show is that this inorganicism is functional—that it is a necessary fictional strategy which derives from Gissing's specific concern with the urbanisation of the unclassed. And more than that, that the fictions which dramatise that concern question the ideology of literature itself, ask how far the "free" values of the imagination have meaning in a world which is structured "organically"—that is, as though it were nature—in the service of capitalism. Reading Gissing is not a comfortable experience. Although it can be said of him, as Benjamin says of the naturalists, that he makes a commodity of misery, the labour in the production of that commodity is an activity determined by its situation in the world of production as a whole. Gissing wrote novels to make a living, and he wrote them about the struggle to make a living in the remote respectable corners of urban society: the motive and the representation are at one, and because they are at one, we can never feel that we can ignore the conditions of production. Gissing is a novelist who demands historical materialist analysis, and that is why he cannot be contained within the canon prescribed as literature. He is the lower middle-class *arriviste* who never makes it to the élite, and so his novels are inaccessible to the élite. Reactionary as they are ideologically, however, they are accessible to anybody who really believes that books can matter to the society that determines them—matter because they mimic and therefore estrange its mechanisms. Gissing is an important writer not merely because he deals with central issues, but also because he writes about them in such a way that those issues are exposed to an extent that is totally demystified.

NOTE

1 Eagleton, "Ideology and Literary Form", in *New Left Review* (1975), no. 90, pp. 81–109. A slightly revised version of this important essay is to be found in the same author's *Criticism and Ideology* (1976).

Index